Horses and Their Wild Relatives

OTHER BOOKS BY DOROTHY HINSHAW PATENT

Animal and Plant Mimicry
Bacteria: How They Affect Other Living Things
Bears of the World
Butterflies and Moths—How They Function
Evolution Goes On Every Day
Fish and How They Reproduce
Frogs, Toads, Salamanders, and How They Reproduce
How Insects Communicate
Hunters and the Hunted—Surviving in the Animal World
The Lives of Spiders
Microscopic Animals and Plants
Plants and Insects Together
Raccoons, Coatimundis, and Their Family
Reptiles and How They Reproduce
Sizes and Shapes in Nature—What They Mean
Weasels, Otters, Skunks and Their Family
The World of Worms

Beetles and How They Live (with Paul C. Schroeder)

The sandy-colored kulan, a type of wild ass, lives in the harsh deserts of Mongolia.

Horses and Their Wild Relatives

Dorothy Hinshaw Patent

Holiday House, New York

Illustration p. 27 from *Horses: The Story of the Horse Family in the Modern World and Through Sixty Million Years of History,* by George Gaylord Simpson. Copyright 1951 by Oxford University Press, Inc.; renewed 1979 by George Gaylord Simpson. Reprinted by permission of the publisher.

Library of Congress Cataloging in Publication Data

Patent, Dorothy Hinshaw.
  Horses and their wild relatives.

  Bibliography: p.
  Includes index.
  SUMMARY: An introduction to the members of the horse
family, once a very large group, of which only a few
closely related species remain.
    1. Equidae—Juvenile literature. 2. Horses—
Juvenile literature. [1. Equidae. 2. Horses]
I. Title.
QL737.U62P37   599.72′5   80-23559
ISBN 0-8234-0383-1

To the individuals and organizations devoting their time to saving endangered species from extinction in the wild—may their efforts succeed.

Contents

One · Horses Are Special, 9

Two · How Horses Came to Be, 19

Three · Return of the Wild Horses, 33

Four · Horses in Freedom, 41

Five · Other Wild Horses, 52

Six · Zebras, 65

Seven · Asses, 86

Eight · Horse Relatives, Ancient and Modern, 97

Glossary, 119

Suggested Reading, 121

Index, 123

Wild mustangs, like this stallion which once roamed the wilds of Colorado, are a symbol of freedom to many people.

One

Horses Are Special

The sight of a sleek and glossy horse galloping across a grassy field, mane and tail streaming freely in the wind, is always breathtaking. Although horses are very familiar, they are special symbols of spirit and freedom in spite of their role as one of humankind's most loyal servants. But even with the great interest in horses, little is written about them as living things—where they came from, how they feed, why they run with such graceful swiftness. The free spirit of horses is greatly admired, yet rarely can we read about horses in freedom—wild horses and horse relatives such as zebras and asses. And what of the more distant relatives of horses—what are they and how do they live?

How horses came to be what they are today is one of the best known examples of evolution's gradual changes yet uncovered. And because horses are so important to humans, we have known something about their lives as tame animals for a long time. But only in the last ten years or so have biologists begun to look at horses and their relatives as wild creatures. Now we can understand something of how these animals live and what makes them such special members of the animal kingdom.

What is a Horse?

The scientific name for the horse family is the Equidae (eh'-quid-ee). While the horse family once was a very large one, today there are only a few closely related species left. The word "species" has a very definite meaning to scientists. When animals belong to one species, it means that they look quite similar and that they will mate with one another in the wild. But it isn't always easy to decide which animals belong together in one species, and sometimes scientists disagree. But we do not need to worry about such differences of opinion about equids (members of the family Equidae). Here we'll avoid such scientific nitpicking and use the simplest and most commonly accepted scheme of dividing equids into species.

Besides the horse itself, there are two species of wild asses and three species of zebras alive today. One kind of truly wild horse may also survive on the remote plains of Mongolia. All these equids have similar life styles, living in open country and feeding mainly on grasses. They can all really be called "horses," since their similarities are so striking. A zebra may look very different from a horse, but if its stripes were removed much of the different look would go with them. While they do not interbreed in the wild, all equids can mate with one another in captivity.

Equids are beautifully adapted to a grass-eating life. All their unique features, the things which make them horse-like, can be related to their special life style. The long, graceful neck and head of the horse are necessary so it can reach the ground with its mouth to eat. Grassy fields and plains are open, exposed areas where horses cannot easily hide from their enemies, so they must be able to run away from them swiftly.

The horse body is perfectly designed for fast running over hard ground. The broad hooves can pound firm, often rough ground without incurring damage. The legs move freely forward and backward but have little side to side motion. This lessens the chances of sprains or twisted joints while the animals are running full tilt away from danger. Along its back, the horse's spine is also rigid, which allows it to withstand the harsh jolting of galloping without injury. The long legs are slim and lightweight, with most of the muscles controlling them located in the shoulders against the body, where they do not have to be lifted up with every stride. Running uses up a great deal of oxygen, and the horse's deep chest contains large lungs which can extract plenty of oxygen from the air.

The Better to See

Before it can run away, a horse must be able to spot its enemies quickly. Horse's eyes are placed high up on its head and way out to the sides so that it can see almost all around, even while its head is down grazing. Only the area straight behind the horse's head is not visible to its watchful eyes. While the pupil of the human eye is round, directing vision straight ahead, the horse's pupil is rectangular, allowing the animal to see to both the front and back at the same time. Because of the way its eyes are shaped, the horse can see the grass close up in clear focus with one part of each eye while it watches the distance, also in good focus, with another part of each eye. This ability enables equids to be watchful for enemies while they are feeding. But it also means that the horse cannot adjust its eyes the way we can. The animal must move its eyes or its head to bring objects at different distances into focus. Because our eyes point straight ahead, we can focus both of them on the same thing at the same time. This "binocular vision" enables us to judge distances very well. The side-pointing eyes of the horse, however, allow only some overlap of vision in front, so horses do not have as much depth perception as humans do.

Horses can also turn their ears this way and that

to listen for sounds coming from different directions. The shape of the ears helps funnel sound into them as well, giving horses great sensitivity to soft, distant sounds. Equids also have a good sense of smell and may sometimes be warned by their noses of danger before their eyes or ears detect it.

Chewing and Digesting

Grass is a very tough food, hard to chew and difficult to digest. For those animals which have evolved the ability to feed on it, it is an abundant and reliable source of food. But any grass-eating animal needs special equipment. Grass contains lots of hard, abrasive silica, a sand-like material. If we ate grass, our teeth would wear down to nothing within months. But horses can eat grass every day of their lives and survive to over thirty years of age.

They can do this because of their special teeth. Our teeth are short. Only the roots which hold the teeth firmly in the jaw extend below the gum line. But a horse's teeth are very long. As the tops of the horse's teeth wear down from chewing grass, the teeth push gradually through the jaw so that there is always the right amount of tooth in the mouth for proper chewing.

The surface of the horse's tooth is different from ours, too. Our incisors, or front teeth, have blade-like edges for cutting off bits of food. Our back teeth—the

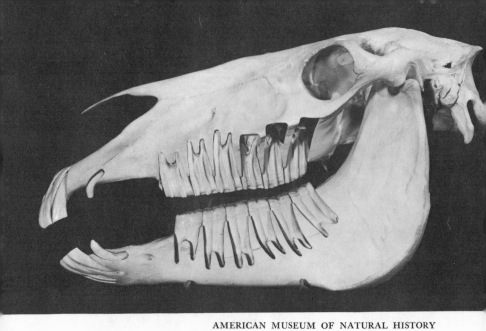

This male horse skull shows the long roots on a horse's teeth. The incisors, at the front of the skull, are used to nip off grass. The small canine teeth behind the incisors are present only in males. Behind the canines is a gap, followed by the broad, chewing premolars and molars.

molars and premolars—have small ridges along the edges and tiny bumps on the surfaces which help us chew our varied foods. The horse also has these same two kinds of teeth. The incisors of a horse, six on top and six on the bottom, have flattened tops with sharp edges. They slant forward rather than pointing upward and downward. Our top teeth close in front of our bottom teeth. But the edges of the horse's incisors meet when the animal closes its mouth. This allows it easily to cut off clumps of grass.

In humans, there are teeth called canines between the incisors and premolars. But in horses, there is a gap behind the incisors before the grinding teeth. One reason for the gap is to lengthen the horse's head so the animal can graze while standing. The gap is useful in domesticated horses, for the bit fits right into it. Male horses have pointed canine teeth which emerge just behind the incisors in front of the gap. These teeth are used in fighting.

The grinding premolars and molars of equids are well suited to their job. The enamel, instead of occurring in small ridges and bumps as in human teeth, is raised up into very high loops and ridges. Between these ridges is another material lacking in our teeth called cement. The cement gives strength to the tall ridges. Since it is not as hard as the enamel, the cement wears down a bit faster. This allows the ridges of enamel to stand out so that they can grind the grass into small pieces. When a horse chews, it moves its lower jaw from side to side, breaking up the grass between the ridges on the top and bottom teeth.

Because of its grassy diet, the horse has a digestive system which is very different from ours. In humans, most digestion occurs in the stomach and small intestine. In the large intestine, nutrients and water are absorbed from the already digested food. In horses, most digestion actually takes place in the large intestine. There, in the enlarged cecum (which in humans is reduced to the tiny and sometimes pesky appendix) and in the enormous colon, most of the digestion takes place. The horse's cecum holds 30 liters (about 7 gallons), while the colon has a capacity twice as large.

While our food is digested chiefly by chemicals called enzymes, which are produced by our bodies, grass is digested mainly by bacteria living in the horse's large intestine. Grass is mainly cellulose, and most animals cannot digest cellulose on their own. Bacteria, however, do make enzymes which can break down cellulose. The bacteria use only some of the nutrients derived from the cellulose. The horse's large intestine absorbs the rest.

Legs for Running

A horse's leg is very different from a human's, yet many of the same bones are found in both. We have five toes and walk on the soles of our feet. But a horse has only one toe, which corresponds to our middle one, on each foot, and walks right on the tip of that one toe. The horse's joint which corresponds to our knee is located way up at the top of its hind leg, and the upper leg bone, called the femur, is actually right next to the body of the animal instead of below it. The horse femur is short and heavy. The horse's front leg is similar. The upper bone, the humerus, is short and strong and is hidden under the body skin.

The part of the horse's leg which we see actually

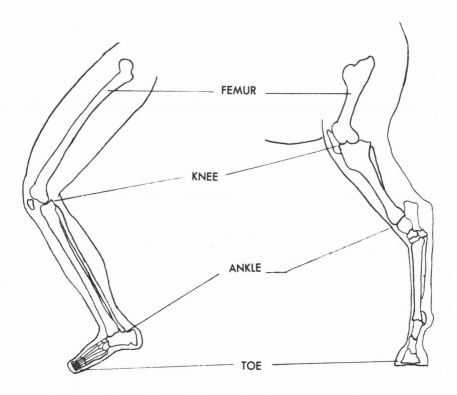

FEMUR

KNEE

ANKLE

TOE

While the horse leg and human leg have many of the same bones, there are big differences between them. DRAWING BY THE AUTHOR

corresponds to the lower part of the human arm or leg. We have two bones next to one another in our lower legs and arms. One of these bones rotates, allowing us to turn our ankles and wrists this way and that. But horses have only one large, strong bone in each upper leg. What is left of the smaller one is fused to the larger one.

What look like the knees on a horse actually correspond to our ankles and wrists. The lower leg bones of the horse are enlarged and strengthened versions of our middle foot and hand bones. The ankle of a horse, which is called the fetlock, represents the joint between the human foot and middle toe on the hind legs, and between the hand and the middle finger on the front legs. Our middle toe and finger each have three small bones connected by two joints. The horse's foot is like our finger. There are three bones, but they are short and strong instead of being long and slim like the finger bones. The last bone forms the core of the horse's hoof, which is really like a huge, overgrown fingernail.

The arrangement of bones in the horse's leg gives it long, strong limbs with a few strong bones. Feet like ours, with so many bones, are quite prone to injury when pounded against the ground for long periods. Large flat feet like ours make swift running impossible, while the horse, perched up on the very tips of its toes, can take off and gallop away in a flash.

Two

How Horses Came to Be

Horses and humans look very different. Yet we can recognize the same bones in the horse and human skeleton and the same parts of the horse and human digestive system. This is because horses and humans are related, despite our obvious differences. Horses and humans, along with cows, rats, cats, dogs, kangaroos, and all other animals which feed their young on milk, are all mammals. They belong to the group which biologists call the "Class Mammalia." If we look far enough back into the past, we can find fossils of animals believed to be ancestors common to all mammals. These common ancestors lived more than 180 million years ago. Between that time and today, many different animals have evolved from those primitive, original mammal ancestors. Some of them still exist today, while others have died out and are extinct.

When we realize that horses are standing on the tips of single, enormously enlarged toes, we wonder how they ever came to be that way. How could their other toes have disappeared? And how did their long teeth, with the high folded ridges of hard enamel, come to be that way? Horses started out with the same ancestors as other mammals. And yet these animals all ended up looking very different.

Evolving and Adapting

To understand how plants and animals came to be the way they are, we must realize that millions of years went into the making of all the different things alive today. Countless generations of animals have been born, lived, reproduced, and died since the first animals appeared on Earth. In each generation, those animals which were able to survive long enough to reproduce passed their inherited traits on to the next generation of their kind. In each generation of any sort of living thing, all individuals are not identical. There are differences in many traits. Some traits may be an advantage in one environment while others might be more suited to a different environment. For example, a thick, heavy coat of fur is useful to an animal living in a cold climate, while this same animal might die of overheating in a warm climate. The woolly mammoths which lived in cold places during the Ice Age had plenty of fur. But the elephants of today, which live in the warm climates of India and Africa, have only a few hairs scattered over their bodies.

So, as the surrounding environment changes, living things must change over the generations or die out. In a hot climate, animals with heavy coats are likely to die before they grow up and reproduce, while animals with thinner coats have a better chance of surviving long enough to pass on their traits to the next generation. Modern horses evolved over millions of years in response to the gradual changes in their environment, from softy marshy ground where juicy, tender plants grew, to open plains covered with tough but abundant grass. Along the way, many sorts of horses developed and died out as others better adapted to new conditions replaced them.

The Dawn Horse

Horses provide one of the very best examples of how animals can change through evolution and adapt to the changing environments around them. Even a close look at the earliest known "horse," eohippus, gives no clue that it could possibly have evolved into modern equids. As a matter of fact, when the first eohippus ("dawn horse" in Greek) skeleton was uncovered in Great Britain, the scientist who described it in 1839 had no idea that he was examining an ancestor of the horse. He thought the skeleton looked rather like that of a somewhat large rodent, called the hyrax. So he gave this new fossil creature the name Hyracotherium, meaning hyrax-like mammal. Many years later, American paleontologists uncovered similar skeletons in the American West. The American scientists did not know that their fossils were the same as Hyracotherium. And since by this time they suspected that the animal they had uncovered was an early ancestor of horses, they gave it the name eohippus. Later, the remains of eohippus and Hyracotherium were compared and found to be similar enough to be placed together. Since the first name given to such animals was Hyracotherium, it had to be kept as the official scientific name. But eohippus, which is a much more appropriate name, is still used informally for this earliest known equid.

Eohippus is so different from a horse that only by looking at the fossils of animals which led from the one to the other can their relationship be recognized. Eohippus was a small animal, only 25 to 50 centimeters (10 to 20 inches) tall at the shoulder. It had four toes on its front feet and three toes on each back foot. Each of these toes had a tiny hoof covering its end. But, unlike a horse, eohippus did not carry its weight on hooves. It had pads on the bottoms of its feet like a dog, and it walked on the pads. Its legs were not as long for the size of its body as are those of a horse. In the upper legs (corresponding to our lower legs and arms) there were still two long bones instead of the one bone of the modern horse. The leg bones of eohippus were arranged so that they still allowed some side to side

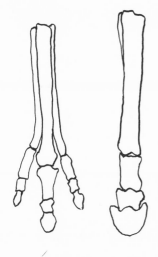

The hind leg of Eohippus had three toes (left) while the modern horse (right) has only one. The bones are drawn as if the two animals were the same size, but Eohippus was much smaller than a horse.
DRAWING BY THE AUTHOR

movement and some rotation, unlike those of present-day horses.

Eohippus had a somewhat flexible, curved spine, more like that of a rabbit or a greyhound than that of a horse. Its tail, too, was more doglike than horselike, for it was quite long. Modern horses have long tails, but they are made up of long hairs. The bony part of a horse's tail is quite short, as you can see if you look at a young foal. The neck of eohippus was not especially long. Its skull had just the beginnings of the gap between the front nipping teeth and the back chewing teeth. The teeth themselves were quite unspecialized. They were more like human teeth than horse teeth. They were short, with low ridges, and showed no sign of the high ridges supported by cement which characterize a horse's teeth.

Eohippus was a very successful animal in its own time. It was quite well adapted to the environment around it. We cannot think of it as an imperfect or undeveloped horse. Horses are adapted to living on open, hard-packed grassy plains. When eohippus first appeared, there was no grass; grass had not yet evolved. There were bushes and trees with juicy leaves to feed on, so eohippus did not need high-ridged teeth which could wear down gradually. The ground was soft and spongy, so eohippus did not need hard hooves. Its padded toes could spread out and support its weight properly on soft ground. The small size of eohippus allowed it to move easily through the bushes and among the trees. An animal as large as a horse would probably have had trouble moving about in the primitive forests where eohippus lived.

Changes With Time

The earliest fossils of eohippus are about 60 million years old. Paleontologists call the period during which eohippus lived the Eocene. The Eocene began about the same time as eohippus appeared and ended about 20 million years later. During the Eocene, eohippus spread out over Europe and North America, which were connected in those days. But around 30 million years ago, the continents separated, isolating the European eohippuses from those in North America. Looking back and knowing what was to happen later, we can see that the horse family in Europe developed only species which eventually died out, while the horse family in North America evolved into some kinds which died out and others which kept evolving into more and more horse-like animals.

During the Eocene period, most of the changes which occurred in horses were in the teeth. In eohippus, the back three teeth on each side of both the upper and lower jaws, the molars, were quite different from the four teeth in front of them, the premolars. The molars were similar to ours—rather square, heavy chewing teeth. Bit by bit, during the Eocene, primitive horses evolved premolars which were more and more like molars. The late Eocene horse called Epihippus had third and fourth premolars which were almost exactly like molars. Thus, at the back of each side of the jaws, Epihippus had a set of five grinding teeth on both the top and bottom, instead of the three grinders of eohippus. The teeth of Epihippus also had somewhat higher and more complex crests and ridges than those of eohippus. The plants were evolving along with the animals which ate them, and their leaves must have been getting tougher to help protect them from being completely eaten up.

Becoming "Horsey"

The geological period after the Eocene is called the Oligocene. During this time, equids which really looked like small horses came into being. These creatures (called Mesohippus) still had three toes on their hind feet, but they also had only three toes on their front feet. They were larger than earlier horses and were already quite well adapted to rapid running. Their legs were long and slim, but they still carried their weight on foot pads rather than on their tiny multiple hooves. Their heads were quite long and horselike, but their muzzles were not so deep as those of modern horses, for their teeth were still short and designed for browsing on leaves rather than grazing on grass. But now there were six grinding teeth in each set, just like in present-day horses. From now on, all six of these teeth would evolve together.

The horses which existed at the end of the Oligocene are called Miohippus. Up to that point, the North American horses had evolved in a fairly straight-line fashion, with one sort evolving into another. There were many different species, to be sure, and some died out without leaving descendants. But there appeared to be one main line of horse evolution with certain tendencies. The animals became gradually larger. The premolar teeth became more and more like molars, and the legs became longer and more adapted to fast running.

But then, at the beginning of the period called the Miocene, about 25 million years ago, several different lines of horses evolved. Most of these animals stuck to

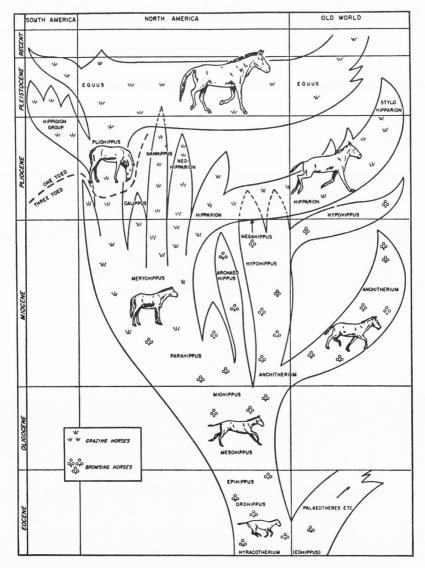

Many kinds of horses have come and gone during evolution. All the browsing horses eventually died out, leaving only grazing horses of the genus Equus alive today.

the original horsey way of life—browsing on leaves in the forest or perhaps along the banks of streams. While horses were evolving and changing here in North America, they had died out in Europe and Asia during the early Oligocene. But now, in the Miocene, another land bridge formed between North America and Eurasia. The highly successful horses of the day, called Anchitherium, marched across and became very common in Europe and Asia. There, like the earlier horses, they underwent their own separate evolution into various sorts of horses.

In North America these "anchitheres" also flourished. A larger sort of horse called Hypohippus evolved from some anchitheres. Hypohippus, in turn, gave rise to some very large horses with strange, spoon-like incisors in the lower jaw. No one knows how these teeth were used. The anchitheres actually represent the ultimate in horse evolution, the main line of which started with the small, browsing eohippus and ended with these larger, stronger, speedier browsers. The line of horse evolution which survived, resulting in the modern horse, was actually a side branch, for it resulted from a change in the feeding habits of the animals, a change away from browsing towards grazing.

Becoming Grazers

During the Miocene period grass was becoming more and more common. Here was an abundant source of food waiting to be utilized, and one branch of the horse family gradually took up grazing. If they hadn't, there would be no horses around today, for the highly successful anchitheres eventually died out, leaving no descendants whatsoever. While the anchitheres and their relatives were living and feeding among the bushes and trees, other descendants of Miohippus were gradually evolving the longer and tougher teeth necessary for feeding on grasses. Their digestive systems also must have been changing so they could digest the grass. Bit by bit, from generation to generation, the teeth of these horses developed more complex crests and ridges of enamel which helped in grinding the grass. The teeth became longer and longer so that they could slowly push out from the jaw as they were worn down.

The cement which fills the spaces between the enamel ridges of horse's teeth also appeared bit by bit. The earliest grazers did not have cement between the crests of their teeth. The cement first appeared as a thin film on the teeth of later grazers. But as the crests became more and more pronounced, the cement layer became thicker and thicker, filling the gaps between the ridges and crests and strengthening the teeth.

These changes in horse teeth occurred in only one line of horse evolution, the one which led to modern horses. The evolution of the horse's teeth from the low, browsing teeth of Miohippus to the high-crowned, grazing teeth of the horse called Merychippus, took place entirely during the Miocene period, over a period

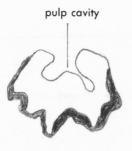

MIOHIPPUS TOOTH   MERYCHIPPUS TOOTH

*The tooth of the early browsing horse, Miohippus, is very dif-
ferent from the tooth of the early grazing horse, Merychippus.
In the Miohippus tooth, the enamel (dark border) merely
covers the dentine (clear center area). The enamel of the
Merychippus tooth forms tall ridges, with softer cement (gray
areas) between them. The dentine is limited to a smaller area,
too.* DRAWING BY THE AUTHOR

of about 15 million years. Fifteen million years is a
long time, yet the evolution of horse teeth was fast
compared to most evolutionary changes.

Merychippus looked very much like a horse. Its
muzzle was deep to make room for its long teeeth. Its
eyes were set high up on its head, like those of our
horses. Some species of Merychippus were 160 centimeters (40 inches) high at the shoulder, as big as some
present-day ponies. The legs of Merychippus were also
more like those of our horses. The two leg bones in the

upper legs were fused into one. This change took away the flexibility of the legs but made them stronger for running.

During the Miocene, the feet of horses also changed. Early Miocene horses had three toes on each foot. But bit by bit the side toes got smaller and the center toe became larger. The foot pads disappeared, too, and the horses began running on the tips of their toes. The hooves of the center toes became larger and stronger. The later kinds of Merychippus looked so much like our horses and zebras that only their tiny side hooves, hanging uselessly like the dew claws of a dog next to the large, central hoof, would give them away.

Modern Horses

From Merychippus onward, the changes leading to Equus, the modern horse, were quite minor. Around five million years ago, Equus horses had evolved in North America and from there spread by land bridges into South America and Eurasia. Horse bones and teeth are among the most common fossils found all over the world except in Australia. And everywhere it went, Equus developed into various species. Some became the zebras of Africa, and others survived as the wild asses of Africa and Asia. Others became the wild horses which would later be tamed by humans and developed into all the modern breeds.

But in their homeland, North America, and in South America, where they had become extremely common, horses mysteriously disappeared. They survived the harsh Ice Ages, only to vanish later. No one knows for sure why all the American horses died off. Some people suggest that some terrible epidemic swept over both continents, wiping all of them out. It is hard to imagine any disease so potent that it could do such a thing.

Other people think that the early Indians, who came across the Bering Strait land bridge and gradually worked their way southward, killed off the horses for food as they went along. This too is hard to imagine, for the Indians were on foot and had only simple weapons like bows and arrows for hunting. There were so many horses and so few Indians that it is hard to believe that these early humans could have killed off all the horses, while other food animals such as antelope, bison, and deer survived in large numbers. The disappearance of horses from America is a mystery which probably will never be completely solved.

Three

Return of the Wild Horses

For over eight thousand years the ringing neigh of the wild stallion was absent from both North and South America. But when Spanish explorers arrived in the 16th century, they brought horses with them. Without their hardy mounts, the conquistadors would never have succeeded in conquering the New World. The Spanish horses were slightly larger than Arabians. Several breeds of horses, including Arabians, went into producing these tough animals, which could survive a rough crossing of the ocean lasting several months and step out onto the dry land of the New World still strong enough to carry a heavy load.

As more and more Spanish explorers, gold-seekers, and settlers arrived in the Americas, the demand for horses increased. Breeding farms were established in Puerto Rico, Cuba, and Santo Domingo, and additional horses, called Barbs, were brought in from North Africa. Some horses escaped into the wild and adapted well to a life of freedom. After all, the grassy plains which covered much of the West were the ideal habitat for these horses, whose ancestors had evolved there.

Indians Discover Horses

In the middle of the sixteenth century, the Spanish explorer Coronado launched a large expedition—250 men and 1,500 animals—across Mexico and northward into the hot southwestern deserts. In his search for golden riches, Coronado pushed as far north as present-day Kansas. But the Indians of the plains had no riches. They lived a nomadic life, traveling from campsite to campsite, taking their few belongings with them on raft-like sleds dragged by dogs. While their ancestors had seen and even hunted horses thousands of years before, the Indians had no knowledge of these animals. They were amazed at the sight of a man on top of a horse, thinking that they were one strange creature.

While Coronado's expedition gave the Plains Indians their first look at horses, it took many years before they learned how to use the animals themselves. The Indians were actually forbidden by Spanish laws to use horses. But in the early seventeenth century, in what is now New Mexico, the authorities began allowing Indians to ride horses and act as herders to help out the Spanish ranchers. Then the knowledge of horse handling passed rapidly from tribe to tribe, and by the middle of the eighteenth century, Indian tribes all the way to the Canadian border had adopted horses and become fine horsemen.

Once they learned that horses were much more valuable as mounts and draft animals than as mere food, the Plains Indians were on the way to a completely new and much richer way of life. Horses became such a vital part of their life style that the American image of these Indians is as superb riders and expert mounted fighters. It is hard to believe that these skills were developed in such a short period of time.

The Indians were also experts in running off the white man's horses, sneaking in at night and stampeding whole herds back to their own camps. During these raids, horses easily became separated from the herd and escaped into freedom. Neither Indians nor white men closely corralled their stock, and many horses wandered off and joined the wild herds. In this way, the stock of wild horses in the American West built up.

Wild horses and Indian ponies were put to use by explorers during the early days of our country. When Lewis and Clark set out to explore the Northwest, they relied a great deal on horses supplied by friendly Indians for much of their transportation. Later explorers, too, depended on Indian horses and on wild horses which had been captured and broken.

More Wild Horses

During the entire period of the settling of the West
and the Indian wars, horses were escaping into the wild.
The new additions to the original Spanish stock, which
were called mustangs, included horses of all sorts, from
small ponies to heavy draft horses. Those which could
survive in the wild interbred with one another, creating a blend which varied from place to place.

In the early nineteenth century, huge herds of wild
horses shared the plains with the bison. At first people
viewed the Great Plains as no more than an obstacle
to cross on the way westward. Wild horses and bison
were shot for sport or food. Before the century was out,
however, settlers came to the plains themselves. Since
the horses and bison were in their way, these animals
were killed off in incredible numbers. At the beginning
of the nineteenth century, sixty million bison roamed
the Great Plains. They passed by in herds numbering
in the thousands. But by the late 1800's, the bison were
almost extinct, killed off by people who could not
make room for wild things in their lives. Most of the
wild horses, too, were killed during this time.

Many bands of wild horses did manage to survive,
however, and have remained to this day. Several populations of wild horses now live in Nevada, Utah,
Wyoming, and Oregon, with a few bands in California,

Idaho, Colorado, and Montana. There is much disagreement about what to do about the wild horses. By the strict definition of the word "wild," the present day mustangs are not truly wild at all. Since they are descended from formerly tame animals, those horses should be called "feral" rather than wild. This distinction is important, for the laws affecting wildlife in the United States provide protection only to the truly wild animals such as deer, elk, bears, and wolves. Since the mustangs are feral rather than wild, they are not affected by laws protecting wildlife.

For many years, feral horses were treated badly. When people thought there were too many of them on the range, they were rounded up, often by aircraft, and sold to slaughterhouses for pet food. Many horses died or were injured during the drives, but any that could still walk and stand were crowded into trucks bound for the slaughterhouses. But as time went by, some people became angry at the way the horses were being treated. These people felt that the wild horses were a vital part of the American West and that they deserved at least as much dignity and consideration as native wildlife species.

The most influential of these friends of the wild horses was "Wild Horse Annie," whose real name was Velma Johnston. She publicized the plight of wild horses and organized horse lovers so that, in 1959, the first law giving some protection to feral horses was established. The Wild Horse Annie Law provided that no aircraft or motorized vehicles be used in wild horse roundups. The law wasn't much, but it was a start. Horse lovers continued to pressure the government until, in 1962, a protected wild horse range was set up in a remote section of government land in Nevada. In 1968, a wild horse range was also established in the Pryor Mountains along the Montana-Wyoming border. In these refuges at least, wild horses would be protected.

When the wild horses in an area become too numerous, the Bureau of Land Management holds roundups. The excess horses are given homes through the "Adopt-a-Horse" progam.
BUREAU OF LAND MANAGEMENT

Most of the wild horses in the United States were still not safe from roundups on horseback or from horse hunters. Anyone could go out and shoot or capture wild horses any time he wanted to as long as no aircraft or motorized vehicles were used. Mrs. Johnston and other horse lovers wanted more than that for the wild horses and their cousins, the feral burros. Finally, in 1971, after much controversy over the proper role of these animals in the West, the Wild Free-roaming Horse and Burro Act was passed. Since that time, all feral horses and burros in the United States have been under the protection of the government. No one can go out and shoot or capture mustangs, except as part of a government program to manage wild horses. The wild burros are protected in the same ways.

Since this law was passed there have been problems managing wild horse and burro populations. Since there are no predators which hunt and kill the wild horses and burros, their populations tend to increase. The rangelands can feed only so many animals, and deer, elk, sheep, and cattle must share the rangelands with the horses. One solution devised by the Bureau of Land Management is the "Adopt-a-Horse" program. When biologists from the BLM feel that there are too many horses living in a particular area, the animals are rounded up. Since October, 1976, helicopters have been allowed in BLM roundups. The excess animals are placed in the care of citizens who promise to take care of them. The adopted horses can be used for riding or breeding, but they cannot be used in any money-making way, such as for rodeo bucking horses. No one person can adopt more than four horses in one year. If the person has cared humanely for an adopted horse for one year, he or she can apply for ownership of the animal. A veterinarian must sign a health certificate for the horse before the person can take ownership.

The Adopt-a-Horse proram has had its problems, but it at least helps solve the problem of what to do with the excess wild horses. It costs the government from $400 to $800 per adopted horse to round them up and arrange the adoption. When roundups are made, any excess horses which are not suitable for adoption must be destroyed, for they cannot be returned to the range without risking starvation for the bands which still live there.

As of July, 1979, more than 12,000 horses had been adopted. In early 1980, the Bureau of Land Management had a three-year backlog of people wanting to adopt wild horses. But with about 50,000 horses to manage, the excess mustangs rounded up could quickly exceed the demand for adoption. For example, in 1980, the state of Nevada, where most mustangs live, wanted to cull out 10,000 animals. If this were done over a short period of time, most of the animals would have to be destroyed.

Four

Horses in Freedom

Most people have some familarity with tame horses. We see photographs of them almost daily, and see them in circuses and cowboy films. We may be lucky enough to enjoy riding horses now and then, or may even own one. But the behavior of a horse which lives around people is very different from that of a wild horse. Tame animals have little chance to show their natural behavior, as do animals such as horses which have evolved to live in small bands out in the open countryside. By studying how horses live in the wild, we can learn much about their true nature. We can understand them better, both as animals with their own sort of character and as our companions. For example, some people look down on horses and say they are stupid animals because they panic when frightened and may not escape a desperate situation such as a barn fire. But when we understand that flight is the natural reaction for a fleet-footed animal with few defenses, which lives in open grasslands, we can see that a strong flight reaction in the face of danger has enabled horses to survive over the ages.

The Wild Horse Family

One place where horses range relatively undisturbed is the Pryor Mountain Wild Horse Range, 43,000 acres set aside for horses along the Wyoming-Montana border. During 1970, a young biologist named James Feist studied the Pryor Mountain horses for six months. Mr. Feist was killed in a plane crash in 1973, but his studies have been published by his professor, Dr. Dale McCullough. Mr. Feist individually identified all 270 horses on the range at that time. He mapped out the wanderings of the different horse bands and studied six of these groups at close range after the horses got used to him, so he could observe their behavior in detail.

Mustangs live in small family groups consisting of one stallion and one to three mares with their young. Stallions without mares live in small bachelor groups; often only two animals travel together. The family bands are quite stable, with the same animals always traveling with each other. The bachelor groups are more likely to change from time to time. Each band has a familiar range over which it travels, and it shares this range with other bands. A band wanders considerably in its search for food and water, with the stallion always

Mustangs live in small family bands like this one. They can survive in areas where few plants live.

controlling, guiding, and protecting his family. He is always on the lookout.

When a stallion senses danger, or the presence of other horses, he gives a warning snort which alerts his band. His family bunches up behind their protector. If he has any doubts about safety, the stallion turns and drives his band away. If any horses are reluctant to run, the stallion drives them on, lowering his head with his ears back and his teeth bared. He sways his neck back and forth with a snake-like motion, his chin sometimes almost touching the ground. If the mare he is herding doesn't take the hint and run where he wants her to go, she may end up with a nip on her flank. No one in the band questions the authority of the stallion.

When Stallions Meet

When two mustang bands encounter one another, the stallions approach each other. They arch their necks and prance, raise their muzzles and roll their eyes, swish their tails and curl their lips. They may walk to a nearby pile of dung and take turns defecating and sniffing at the pile. The pile of dung may provide scent clues which give the stallions information about one another. They may push one another around a bit or even kick, but usually such encounters are not serious. Then the stallions return to their bands and keep them apart. At a water hole, Mr. Feist saw as many as five bands nearby at one time, each waiting its turn. When one band left, another would walk down to drink.

Most of the time, the various horse families tolerate one another without much fuss. Besides taking turns at water holes, the bands share dusting places. These spots are sometimes created by the horses by pawing at the dry ground and loosening the soil. Sometimes the animals in one band have a "rolling party," each horse rolling in the dust in turn, the stallion last. Water holes are also used as rolling places, especially by stallions. Sometimes the horses get so completely covered with mud that they can be recognized only by the band they are with.

Once in a while, stallions get into fights over mares. One stallion may try to steal a mare from another, who defends her fiercely. The two stallions approach one another, prancing elegantly forward with arched necks, ears pointed forward, and tails slightly raised. They touch noses, loudly sniffing, sometimes letting out a squeal and pawing at the ground. Bit by bit they sniff each other, working their way along their necks and bodies. They sniff especially intensely at the flanks, with snorts which can be heard from some distance.

Young mustang stallions often play-fight with each other, like these Pryor Mountain horses are doing. In this way they develop the fighting skills which they will use later when they have their own family bands. ALAN J. KANIA

Once the sniffing is over, the real fight begins. The stallions rear at one another, often sinking their teeth into one another's necks. The fight is punctuated by piercing squeals. During the fight, the stallions may separate and display themselves by prancing parallel to each other with arched necks and gracefully lifted feet. They may take turns adding to a dung heap. During the whole dramatic scene, the mares wait passively, sometimes feeding, paying little or no attention to the fight. A stallion fight ends when one animal has had enough and runs off. The other may follow in hot pursuit, trying to bite at the fleeing tail. But often the fight merely ends quietly, with the two animals returning to their bands.

Life in the Band

The horses in a band are like an extended family. While they quarrel now and then with laid-back ears, nips, and occasional kicks, they generally get along quite well. The mares watch out for their foals, letting them nurse whenever they want. If a mare is separated from her foal, she gives a low, searching whinny. She threatens any horse which comes too close to her baby and stands between the foal and any possible threat. The stallion also watches out for the foals, herding them protectively and guiding them back to the band if they get separated. If the mother has trouble shield-

T. H. CLUTTON-BROCK

These Highland ponies are carefully grooming one another with their teeth.

ing her foal from another horse, she lets out a whinny, bringing the stallion to the rescue. He herds the other horse away from the foal.

A favorite activity of all herd members except the stallion is mutual grooming. While the acts of rolling in the dust, scratching on branches, and reaching around and nibbling with its own teeth help a horse remove some dead skin and loose hair, it is evident that some parts of the body just cannot be kept clean without the help of other horses. When a horse wants to be groomed, it approaches a resting animal in a friendly fashion and the two touch noses, sniffing gently. They then step forward a bit and sniff necks. Then they begin to nibble at one another, removing dead hair and skin with small, firm bites. Sometimes their teeth can be heard clacking away as they work along the necks, across the shoulders, along the sides, and down to the tails. Grooming may take only a couple of minutes or it may last for a quarter of an hour. Once they reach the tails, often the animals switch and groom down their opposite sides, again working from neck to tail. Grooming not only helps keep the skin healthy, it also reinforces the friendly feelings between animals in the herd.

The horses in the band communicate with one another in various ways. The snort of a stallion or alerted mare warns of possible danger. The whinny is often a call for help, given by a lost foal or its mother or by a mare needing the stallion's aid in chasing off a mare too close to her foal. If a playful foal wanders off while romping with a youngster from a different band, the stallion will neigh for it to return. Stallions will also whinny back and forth when challenging one another.

The nicker is a soft sound, used as a friendly, close

greeting. A mare will nicker when reunited with her foal, and a stallion will nicker to a mare. Domesticated horses use this greeting for their human friends.

Horses have various ways of showing displeasure with one another. Often the first sign of annoyance is laying the ears back along the neck. If this doesn't get the point across, the threatening horse may swing its head back and forth, opening its mouth and pulling its lips back to show its teeth. Ignoring this obvious warning may result in a bite. Horses also use kicks. If another horse comes too close, a mare that doesn't want to be disturbed may raise a hind leg threateningly. If the other horse comes too close anyway, it may get a kick.

Growing Up Fast

Foals may look like awkward creatures, but they are amazingly strong and able from the time they are born. Like most other animal babies, foals are born in the springtime, when food is abundant and will be for a few months. The young horse is born with its eyes open. Just about the first thing it tries to do is stand up on its long, wobbly legs. First the foal stretches out its front legs and gets into a sort of sitting position. The tricky part is to get its stiff hind legs to work so that they will support its weight reliably. After a tough beginning, the foal is able to walk, nurse, follow its

mother, make sounds, and react to its mother—all by
the time it is only two hours old. In just half a day, it
can trot and gallop about.

During the first few days after her foal is born, the
mother is very protective. She will not let another horse
get close and always puts her body between her baby
and other horses. During those early days, the foal
is still developing its attachment to its mother, and it
is still gaining strength and getting used to the world.
As long as it stays close to its mother, the foal is safe.

During its first week, the foal remains within a few

*The mare is very protective of her foal. This mother Prze-
walski horse is warning that she means business by laying her
ears back.* ZOOLOGICAL SOCIETY OF LONDON

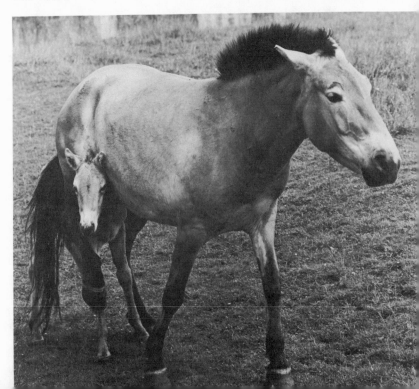

feet of its mother nearly all the time. Gradually, the youngster gains confidence and spends more and more time away until, by the time it is five months old, the foal is near its mother only half the time. The first moves away are small play trips; the foal gallops away from its mother and heads right back. As it gets older, the foal plays with other youngsters from its own band, galloping off with them and having mock fights. If there are no other foals to play with, the lone foal may try to get its mother to play or may toss objects into the air like a puppy.

Although young foals get nearly all their nourishment by suckling their mothers, they start nibbling at grass during the first few days after birth, reaching their muzzles awkwardly down between their long front legs. As they get older, they spend more and more time feeding on grass. By the age of one year, a young horse may spend as much as three-quarters of its waking hours grazing. Some foals have a close relationship with their mothers which may last as long as four years, while others become independent much earlier. Even when a mare gives birth when her prior offspring is a year old, the older foal may stay near its mother and share her place in the band. If two young horses travel with their mother, the youngest foal stays close by her side while the older one stays a bit behind.

Five

Other Wild Horses

Horses and humans have been companions for centuries. Yet the spirit of the wild sleeps in the domesticated horse, ready to be awakened if by chance the animal should become free. Around the world, tame horses have escaped or been released into the wild and have thrived there. Today, wild horses live in Japan, Australia, Nova Scotia, South America, the United States, and many European countries. Some of these horses are partially domesticated; once a year or so some horses are removed from the herd and tamed. But others live in complete freedom, undisturbed unless they become pests to people. A few of these wild animals are thought to be remnants of the original ancestors of domesticated horses.

Although the ancestry of today's feral and half-wild horses varies greatly, they behave in a remarkably similar fashion. Like the mustangs in the Pryor Mountain Wild Horse Range, feral horses elsewhere live in harem bands led by a single stallion, and in bachelor herds. The mares remain in the same band for years, and young mares as well as young stallions tend to leave their own families as they mature. While the stallion completely dominates the family in the Pryor Mountain horses, mares take on more important roles, such as leading the band to water or away from danger, in many semi-wild horse populations. The mares also often have their own ranking system, with one mare dominating the others, another mare second in status, and so forth on down to the last mare at the bottom of the pecking order. Male horses are removed from these half-wild herds frequently, which may help explain the greater social role of the mares.

Feral horses are tolerated and occasionally rounded up and broken in for human use in Japan, Argentina, Australia, Germany, and Sweden. But perhaps the best known and most romantic feral horses outside the United States are the horses of the Camargue, in southern France. These small, strong animals are descended from Arab horses which went wild about 2,000 years ago, during the Roman occupation of what was then called Gaul. The Camargue horses have developed wide, hard hooves for running on the marshy ground of their homeland. These hardy creatures live in the delta of the Rhone River, among the marshes and scrub brush country bordering the sea. Way back in 1550, a head count showed about 4,000 mares living in the Camargue. Today there are only about 750. While the animals are owned and branded, they are allowed to roam free most of the year. Camargue mares are essentially wild, for only young males are roped, tamed, and ridden. No one in the Camargue will ride a mare.

Like most other feral horses, Camargue horses live in small family bands. But these bands do not necessarily stay separate all year around. During the summer months, after the breeding season is over, several bands may join up to form a large herd. The animals in the herd travel together, but still maintain the separation of their family groups. Apparently, horses living in the large herds suffer much less from the annoying and painful bites of insects such as horseflies, midges, and mosquitoes which are especially common in marshy areas like the Camargue.

The Camargue horses are born a gleaming black or dark brown, but gradually lighten in color as they get older. The fully mature animals are pure creamy white. Because they are familiar with humans, the Camargue horses make good subjects for scientific studies and for photography. Some of the most beautiful horse photographs have been of these spirited creatures galloping through the waters of the marshes or fighting one another for possession of a harem.

Island Ponies

Islands dot the Atlantic coast of North America, and several of them are inhabited by wild ponies. Sable Island, off the coast of Nova Scotia, is a treeless wisp of land only about 32 kilometers (20 miles) long and from .8 to 1.6 kilometers (½ to 1 mile) wide. But on this island live over 200 hardy and often beautiful ponies, famous for their flowing manes and tails. Sable Island is called the Graveyard of the Atlantic, for over 200 shipwrecks have occurred there. The Sable Island ponies are almost certainly the descendants of survivors of one or more of these wrecks. During the winter, Sable Island ponies grow long, shaggy coats which protect them from the cold, icy Atlantic winds. The individual family bands come together and travel in larger herds which offer more protection than do the small groups.

The most famous island ponies are the Chincoteague ponies, named for an island off the coast of Virginia. The Chincoteague ponies are said to be the descendants of Spanish horses which swam to shore after a shipwreck over 300 years ago. Indian ponies which escaped to the island could just as easily be their ancestors. Actually, these animals do not live on Chincoteague Island at all, but rather on a smaller, less inviting outer island called

USDA-SCS PHOTO BY DON SCHUHART

These Chincoteague ponies are enjoying the peace and quiet of Assateague Island where they live most of the year.

Assateague. Every July, the ponies are herded from Assateague to Chincoteague for an auction during which some of the foals of the season are sold to the highest bidders. The money from the sale is used to manage the horses and to support the Chincoteague

Volunteer Fire Department. Tourists from all over the eastern states come to see the ponies swim from one island to the other and gallop down the main street of town to the corral where they are kept until the auction is over. The foals which are auctioned are still quite young, and it is hard for them and their mothers to be separated. After the auction, the ponies are freed for their return to Assateague, where they live in freedom until the next Pony Penning Day the following July.

British Half-Wild Ponies

In the rugged hills and moors of the British Isles live nine different breeds of ponies which spend most of their time living free from disturbance. The largest breed, called the Dales pony, is almost big enough to be called a horse while the smallest, the Shetland pony, is half as high at the shoulder.

We think of Shetland ponies as being tame mounts just the right size for children to ride. But in its homeland, the Shetland is left to its own devices all year around, except for valuable breeding stallions, which may be sheltered during the wintertime. Shetlands roamed wild for hundreds of years until the late nineteenth century, when selective breeding was used to establish a typical kind of pony. Shetlands may be any color. While pintos are often seen here in the United

States, black animals are favored in Britain. Shetlands are lovely animals, with strong bodies, wide faces, and long flowing manes and tails.

Other breeds of half-wild British ponies include the Welsh mountain pony, the Connemara, Highland,

The British Isles are home to many types of half-wild ponies, like these two Highland ponies.   T. H. CLUTTON-BROCK

New Forest, Dartmoor, and Fell ponies. Most of these ponies are owned. Some are left out year around, but others are brought in during the winter. The breeding stallions are sometimes selected, and the young colts may be taken out of the herds during fall roundups and sold.

The Exmoor pony is one of the oldest breeds known. Wild ponies have roamed the area for perhaps as long as 100,000 years, and some horse experts believe that Exmoor ponies are basically unchanged from prehistoric times. This would make them true wild horses. These extremely hardy animals are a light tan or brownish color, with a light-colored muzzle and dark legs, mane, and tail. They have a thick coat, and foals are protected from harsh weather by a woolly undercoat. The Exmoor ponies are rounded up each fall and inspected, but they live a life of freedom the rest of the year.

Domestic Horse Ancestry

The Exmoor pony may be a surviving variety of truly wild horse and possibly an ancestor of other British ponies found today. But what were the other ancestors of present-day horses? The many breeds of modern horses have ancestors which were at one time wild, and horse experts have spent a great deal of time trying to figure out what these ancestors were like.

Even up to a couple hundred years ago, wild horses roamed over much of eastern Europe and western Asia. One sort of wild horse was called the tarpan. The steppe tarpan was a small, dark gray horse which lived in Russia. It had a thick head, long pointed ears, and a frizzy mane. Steppe tarpans seem to have lived in small family herds led by a protective stallion, just like other horses. They were fleet of foot, difficult to catch, and hard to tame. Horses thought by some to be re-created steppe tarpans live in some zoos (such as the Brookfield zoo in Chicago and in the Catskill Game Park in New York) today. These animals were obtained by crossing certain ponies and then breeding them with Przewalski horses.

The forest tarpan was similar to the steppe tarpan but smaller and less stocky. It had a very lightly colored winter coat. Forest tarpans lived in the forests of Poland and Russia. Up until the early 1800's, a few forest tarpans still roamed the Bialowiecz forest of Poland. Then they were rounded up and sent to a zoo. Because they reproduced too rapidly, they were shot, used in cruel Roman-style combats with wild animals, or given away to local peasants. In recent years, the Polish government became interested in reestablishing the forest tarpan to its rightful habitat. Many of the native Polish ponies called Koniks, believed to be al-most pure-blooded descendants of forest tarpans, were bought and bred to produce horses at least very similar

These Polish horses, which live in freedom on a forest pre-
serve, come as close to the extinct forest tarpan as any horse
alive today. The foals tend to be lighter in color than the
adults, which have dark manes and tails.

BOTH PHOTOS, MAGDALENA JAWOROWSKA

to the original forest tarpan. Now these animals live again peacefully in protected Polish forests. They are attractive animals, with tan coats, dark mane and tail, and dark coloring around their ears. Some have dark legs and some have a stripe down the back leading to the tail, like many other wild equids.

These horses live in famly bands with one stallion and four to eight mares and their offspring. The stallions seem to be especially ready to fight, and a young stallion may enlist the aid of the other young stallions in ousting a harem stallion. In general, however, their behavior fits the pattern for wild horses which we have already learned about.

The Przewalski horse is a true species of wild horse. Even so, the herds found in zoos and animal parks may not be absolutely pure. Always, with wild horses, the problem exists of stallions stealing domesticated mares and adding them to their harems. Then the traits of the domestic stock become mixed with the characteristics of the wild horses.

The typical Przewalski horse is larger and heavier than a tarpan. Its head is stouter and its neck is thicker. It may be a light yellowish gray in color or a lovely reddish brown. It has a light ring around each eye and a light muzzle with dark lower legs, a dark stripe along the back, and a dark, short mane and dark tail. In winter, these inhabitants of the harsh Mongolian plains grow long, protective winter coats.

The heavy head and dark markings are easy to see on this Przewalski mare and her foal. Notice, too, the lack of a forelock.

Because it lived in such an inhospitable and remote land, the Przewalksi horse survived into modern times. For the same reason, we do not know for sure if there are any of these animals left in the wild. Up to the early 1960's, small herds were now and then sighted by parties of hunters. The animals are protected by law, which provides for a five-year sentence for killing one. But laws are hard to enforce in remote areas, and no confirmed sightings of wild Przewalski horses have been made for many years now. We can only hope that a few have managed to survive, far from the influence of humans.

Fortunately, quite a few of these fine animals do live in captivity. When they are kept as family bands in large paddocks, Przewalski horses behave much like feral horses. The stallion is very protective of his mares and rounds them up aggressively. If they are kept in a small enclosure, the stallion sometimes kills mares while trying to herd them. Przewalski horses groom one another enthusiastically, especially in summer while shedding their heavy winter coats.

All breeding in captive herds is recorded, and every year there are more and more Przewalski horses. In 1964 there were 110 and by 1972 there were almost 200 individuals found in 42 different zoos around the world. The main breeding centers for Przewalski horses are in Prague, Czechoslovakia, and in the Catskill Game Park in New York State.

Six

Zebras

Zebras, with their flashy striped coats, are a familiar part of the animal world. But, despite this surface familiarity, most people know very little about these beautiful wild horses. The sight of a few zebras peacefully munching hay in a zoo enclosure cannot compare to the spectacle of hundreds of them grazing in freedom on the African plains.

The zebras's stripes are so striking they would seem to make the animal stand out from its surroundings. But on the grassy plains, the stripes break up the outline of the zebra. They make it hard to tell where the zebra begins and ends, especially when a whole herd of zebras is galloping off together when chased by lions or wild hunting dogs. All the different sets of bouncing stripes, moving this way and that, are very difficult to sort out. Zebra stripe patterns are as individual as human fingerprints. Each zebra has its own unique design. This makes it easy for the animals to recognize one another on sight.

This photo of Burchell's zebras drinking shows how their stripes make it hard to tell where one zebra ends and another begins.

Most scientists agree that there are three distinct species of zebras. The largest of all wild equids is the Grevy's zebra, which lives in parts of Ethiopia, Kenya, and Somalia. If its stripes were taken away, the Grevy's zebra would look more like an ass than a horse, for it

The handsome head of the Grevy's zebra, with its fine stripes and big ears, is very distinctive.

ZOOLOGICAL SOCIETY OF LONDON

has large ears and a thick neck. The voice of the Grevy's zebra is much like a donkey's bray, and its social life resembles that of the African ass more than that of horses and other zebras. The handsome narrow head of the Grevy's zebra is quite distinctive, with its narrow stripes and clusters of long, sensitive hairs around the muzzle.

The plains, or Burchell's, zebra is the most abundant wild equid. It lives in eastern and south-eastern Africa, with some populations in the southwest. Presently there are about 300,000 plains zebras in the wild, many of them protected in wildlife parks. The plains zebra is known by several different names—Grant's, Boehm's, Chapman's, and Damara zebra—for its stripe pattern varies from place to place. The farther south these zebras are found, the less prominent the stripes. Some plains zebras have faint "shadow stripes" between the darker stripes. The plains zebra lives in family groups much like wild horses and has a peculiar barking voice, with a two-or three-syllable "kwa-ha-ha" call resembling neither a neigh or a bray.

The two varieties of mountain zebra live in South Africa. They are more streamlined than plains zebras, with thinner legs and body and narrower hooves, which are better adapted to their more hilly, rocky habitat. The mountain zebra lives in family groups like the plains zebra and has a more horse-like, neighing voice.

Even while drinking at a waterhole, plains zebras stay together in their small family groups.

The Plains Zebra Family

Thanks to Dr. Hans Klingel and his wife, we know more about the life of the plains zebra than of any other wild equid. Like both wild and feral horses, the plains zebras live in tightly-knit family bands and in stallion groups. The family band consists of a harem stallion and one to a few mares with their offspring. In areas where zebras thrive, there may be as many as 16 zebras

Rarely does a photographer capture the birth of a zebra on film. The plains zebra mare (above) has just given birth to her foal, while another mare grazes with her year-old foal in the background. After the foal is born (below), the mare sniffs it and cleans it up. By the time the foal is only six hours old (right), it is able to keep up with its mother. DR. HANS KLINGEL

in one family group. The adult mares belong to the same family as long as they live, and the members of the family look out for one another. If a foal becomes lost, all the mares and the stallion will search for it until found, and the stallion will search for any lost mares. Each stallion looks out for his own mares and does not try to steal adult mares away from other stallions. However, when a young mare is first ready to mate, stallions from nearby herds compete for her attentions and try to cut her out from her family band. Her father tries to fight them off, but there are so many rivals that this is impossible, and eventually a stallion succeeds in making off with her. Usually, she is stolen several times by one stallion and then another before things calm down. The next time she is ready to mate, the whole process may start again. By the time the mare is two and a half years old, she finally becomes a

permanent member of one family group.

A young stallion stays with his father's family for several years, sometimes until he is four years old. He may leave earlier if his mother has a new foal and there are no other young stallions in the group for playmates. If his father dies or becomes old or sick and is replaced by another stallion, the son will also leave and join a stallion band. The Klingels observed an interesting case of this loyalty to the father once when they tranquilized a herd stallion. Another stallion temporarily took over the tranquilized zebra's family, and an adolescent male immediately left the group. Once the original stallion had recovered from the tranquilizer, he reclaimed his family and the other stallion left peaceably. Once his father was back in command, his young son returned, too.

Every animal has its place in the plains zebra family. The herd stallion is "top dog," and the mares have a pecking order. One mare is dominant over the others. When the herd is migrating or running from danger, she leads the group while the stallion takes up the rear. The second-ranking mare travels second in line and so on, down to the lowest-ranking mare. The foals and young zebras follow their own mothers, with the youngest one keeping closest to its mother's side. If a mare of lower rank tries to walk in front of a higher-ranking female, she is threatened or even attacked until she takes her proper place.

Stallions Live Together

The stallion groups are less closely knit than the families. All the adult stallions in the group are of equal rank, while the younger males do have a dominance order similar to that of mares. An adult stallion leads the group. When a stallion is five or six years old, he begins to get interested in starting his own family. He may do so by successfully courting a young mare and defending her against the other stallions, or he may be able to take over the family of an old or sick family stallion. If a family stallion is losing control of his harem, a bachelor may hang around and take over bit by bit, usually without a fight.

Plains zebra bands share the land with one another. They have no specific territories and may join up temporarily when migrating or when running from danger. Usually, however, the bands keep their distance from one another, each grazing or traveling in its own close formation some yards from the nearest other band. The stallion groups tend to stay around the outer edges of a large herd, with the family bands in the center. When the animals are on the move, the stallion groups stay near one another towards the rear or sides of the herd. The family stallions will not tolerate nearby bachelors and will run at them threateningly if they come too near.

A large herd of plains zebras is actually made up of small family groups and stallion groups, as this photo shows.

Each band has a fairly large home range over which it wanders in search of food and water, depending on rainfall and the season. These animals thrive best when there is moderate rainfall. In recent years, heavy rainfall in Kruger National Park in South Africa has encouraged tall grasses and shrubs. Zebra populations have declined there, probably because lions and other predators such as hyenas and leopards can more easily hide and surprise zebras. When the plants are tall and thick it is also more difficult for the zebras to see one another and stay together. Individuals can become separated from the group more easily and thus be more vulnerable to attack.

Fighting Off Enemies

The family spirit of the plains zebra extends to defense against enemies. There is always at least one animal standing guard over the band, keeping watch while the others rest. If danger threatens, the group runs off, with the stallion taking up a protective position at the rear, where he can attack if the enemies get too close. Wild hunting dogs, which live in packs on the plains, usually avoid zebras, probably because of their large size and superior defenses. But a few packs have come to specialize in hunting zebras, and scientists have watched how the dogs and zebras interact with one another.

When a dog pack approaches a zebra family, the dogs bunch together and walk very slowly towards their intended prey. The zebras stand and watch the dogs, often letting them get within 25 meters (81 feet) before they take off. Once the zebras are running, the stallion falls behind the others and kicks backwards at the dogs or turns around and chases them. As the zebras run, they pick up nearby family groups which run with them so that the dogs may eventually be chasing 200 zebras. As long as the zebras stay close together there isn't much the dogs can do to get at them. But if one animal falls behind, the dogs go after it. They jump at the zebra's hindquarters and shoulders and try to get a grip on its muzzle. Even then, the attacked zebra may have a chance. Once, while biologists were watching a pack of dogs attacking a lone mare, they heard the thundering of hooves. Over a rise in the ground appeared the rest of her family band, which galloped full tilt towards the attacking dogs. The zebras ran up to the mare, surrounded her, and galloped off, leaving the dogs hungry and frustrated.

The Sad Case of the Quagga

The loveliest of zebras is no longer with us. With its reddish-brown coat, striped only on the head, neck, and front quarters, and its white belly, legs, and flowing tail, the quagga was indeed a handsome animal. Some experts consider the quagga as a subspecies of the plains zebra, with its reduced striping the extreme of the reduction in stripes from north to south. Others believe that there are significant differences in the skeleton between quaggas and true plains zebras, so that the two should be thought of as separate species. Quaggas and plains zebras are said to have lived together in some areas without interbreeding. This, too, would be evidence that they were distinct species.

Quaggas were abundant during the 18th century as Boer settlers spread across South Africa. The settlers slaughtered the quaggas by the hundreds for their hides and meat. By the late 1870's, quaggas were already extinct in the wild, and the last captive died in the Amsterdam zoo in 1883. Quaggas were especially gentle for zebras, and some were successfully tamed and used in harness. Some say the quagga might have been domesticated and trained if it hadn't been slaughtered. Since zebras are immune to many diseases which attack horses in Africa, tame zebras might have come in handy indeed. But because of the greed and thoughtlessness of the early South African settlers, we will never know either the beauty or the usefulness of this once plentiful creature. All that is left of the quagga is a few skeleton, skins, skulls, and photographs.

This lonely quagga in the London Zoo died in 1872.
ZOOLOGICAL SOCIETY OF LONDON

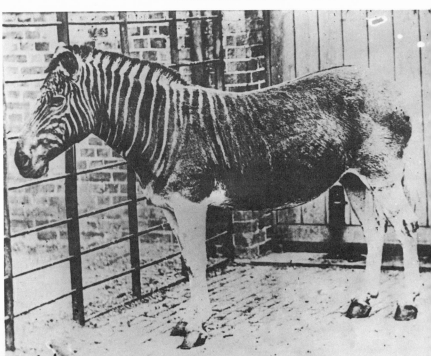

This Hartmann's mountain zebra stallion stands guard while the rest of his family band drinks.

Mountain Zebra Life

The mountain zebra seems to live much like the plains zebra, with family bands and stallion groups. These animals, however, are less sociable with other animals. While groups of plains zebras are often mixed with herds of wildebeeste, mountain zebras keep their distance from other animals. They can survive drier conditions than plains zebras and may go for three days without drinking. While traveling, the stallion may lead the group instead of taking up the rear, and at water holes he will keep watch while the mares drink, taking his own turn last.

The mountain zebra is smaller than other zebras and has a dewlap (a fold of loose, hanging skin) under its neck. Two varieties of mountain zebra exist—Cape mountain zebra and Hartmann's mountain zebra. Hartmann's zebra has narrow black stripes with off-white stripes between, while the Cape mountain zebra has wide, closely spaced black stripes with white ones between. The Cape mountain zebra is smaller and stockier than Hartmann's, with longer ears, narrower hooves, and a more prominent dewlap.

The Cape mountain zebra barely escaped the fate of the quagga. The South African settlers slaughtered

The Cape mountain zebra has wider black stripes than the Hartmann's mountain zebra and is smaller. **DR. HANS KLINGEL**

these hardy animals as well as quaggas, and by 1937 only a few were left. The South African government decided that the animals should be protected, and the Mountain Zebra National Park was established. However, there was one serious problem with the location of the park—within its boundaries were only six mountain zebras, one mare and five stallions! By 1950 there were no mountain zebras left there to protect.

Fortunately a few ranchers in the area had kept mountain zebras on their property, and in 1951 eleven animals were donated to the park. By 1956 this meager herd had increased to 17, and in 1964 another batch of 43 animals were donated by another family. Today over 100 zebras live in this protected area, with a few additional animals still surviving in unprotected areas and in zoos.

Hartmann's zebra is more abundant than the Cape mountain zebra, but it, too, is considered endangered. There are a few thousand remaining animals, some living in protected areas, but others being ever more restricted in their movements by gameproof fencing put up by farmers, which sometimes cuts the zebras off from water. Hartmann's zebras perform a service to other wildlife in their arid habitat. They enter canyons and sniff out water below the surface of dry creek beds. The zebras paw the ground, creating holes which fill with fresh water.

A Grevy's zebra stallion will tolerate other zebras in his territory. The group of zebras in the background is a casual mixed group, not a family unit.

Grevy's Zebra

The plains and mountain zebras and the quagga are all closely related species. The Grevy's zebra, on the other hand, resembles other zebras mainly in its striped coat. It is a significantly larger animal. While plain's zebras stand less than 125 centimeters (50 inches) at the shoulder, an average Grevy's zebra is over 135 centimeters (54 inches) in shoulder height. Many experts believe the Grevy's zebra represents a primitive sort of horse, little changed since the early days of one-toed horses. Other zebras, horses, and asses are thought by these experts to be more closely related to one another. But other scientists believe that the Grevy's zebra is actually more highly evolved than the other zebras, rather than more primitive.

Its social behavior as well as its appearance sets the Grevy's zebra apart from its striped cousins. While both plains and mountain zebras have close, long-lasting family ties, Grevy's zebras have almost no lasting social relationships. Only the mare and her foal care for each other. While Grevy's zebras may be found in small or large herds, these herds shift membership from one hour to the next and may consist of mares, foals, and stallions in just about any combination. When the animals migrate in search of water, almost any animal may lead, and the leader may change frequently as the herd moves along.

The only sort of permanent social arrangement other than the bond between the mare and her foal is the establishment of extremely large breeding territories by a few stallions. These territories, which may have boundaries as long as 10 kilometers (about 6 miles) along one side, are the largest found in any animal. During the dry season, when the other Grevy's zebras migrate to find water, the territorial stallions stay in their homes. They only leave if it is extremely dry. The stallions do not normally defend their territories. They patrol the borders and mark certain key spots along the borders with large piles of dung.

When a mare in mating condition is in a stallion's territory and wanders towards the border, he will try to keep her within its boundaries. If she reaches the edge, the stallion will fight with his neighbor over the mare while both males try to make the mare walk towards

When a Grevy's zebra mare ready to mate approaches the boundary between two stallion territories, the stallions will fight over her. DR. HANS KLINGEL

Grevy's and Burchell's zebras are often seen grazing together in the few areas where both species are common, like Samburu Game Reserve in northern Kenya.

the center of his territory. Once she chooses one territory or the other, the fight ends and the winner follows the mare, while the loser stands at the boundary. These fights over mares are very predictable and were used by Dr. Klingel and his associates to map out the stallion's territories. The researchers would use a jeep to drive a mare across the plains. They could then tell when she reached a territorial boundary by the fight between the stallions as she was about to cross it.

Any other zebras are tolerated in the territories, and males without territories do not attempt to mate with the mares there. The mating terriories allow for peaceful mating of the zebras. Once Dr. Klingel observed a mare which was in mating condition outside any of the territories. Several stallions were nearby, all fighting over her. All the competition and commotion made mating impossible. But when the mare walked into a nearby territory, she was able to mate with its owner in peace.

Seven

Asses

Unfortunately, the terms "ass" and "jackass" have come to mean someone foolish or stupid. Wild asses, as well as tame ones, are not foolish or stupid animals at all. Wild asses manage to survive, despite competition with livestock and human guns, in some of the most uninviting desert regions on Earth. The kulan, a variety of Asiatic ass, can run as fast as 64 kilometers per hour (40 mph), faster than a record-setting thoroughbred. The kiang, another Asiatic ass, can see a human figure nearly a mile away and can catch a scent at 538 meters (500 yards).

African Wild Asses

The least horse-like of equids is the African wild ass, ancestor of the domesticated donkey. These animals have high, narrow hooves suited to maneuvering in their rocky, desert homes. They are very hardy animals, able to tolerate temperatures which soar to 50° C.

(125° F) and capable of surviving two or three days without water. Their gray color blends in with the desert rocks and pale desert plants, and their large ears are attuned to the slightest sound floating on the dry wind.

African asses come in two varieties. The handsome Somali wild ass has a dark, short mane, dark tips on its ears, and delicate stripes around its slender legs. Some Somali asses have a stripe across their shoulders as well, and all have a stripe along the back which often fades out in the middle. The coat may take on a tan or yellow cast in the summer, turning grayer during the winter. The Somali ass is considered an endangered species, but these animals still do run wild in remote areas of Somalia and Ethiopia.

The Nubian wild ass is similar to the Somali, but lacks stripes on its legs. All individuals appear to have the stripe across the shoulders and have a complete, bold stripe down the back. The summer coat of the Nubian ass may be reddish, and it is smaller than its Somali cousin. The Nubian ass, which once inhabited a large area from the Red Sea coast, across the Nile River and through the deserts of Ethiopia and the Sudan, is probably completely extinct in the wild today.

Because they are very wary and fleet of foot, African asses are difficult for scientists to investigate. Dr. Klingel, however, was able to study some animals briefly in Ethiopia. His observations indicate that the African ass has a social life similar to that of Grevy's zebra. Some males have large territories, perhaps even larger than those of Grevy's zebra, and the only close social unit is the mare with her foals.

Asiatic Wild Asses

Asiatic wild asses are more horse-like than their African cousins, so some biologists give them the unfortunate name "half-asses." Asiatic asses have especially long, lower leg bones, which give them slender, graceful limbs and make them capable of especially swift running. These alert and beautiful equids are of two main varieties, the kiang and the onager. Some biologists consider the two as separate species, while others lump them together as the Asiatic wild ass. This hardy species once lived over an enormous range from China across central Asia into India and through Persia (Iran) to Syria and Palestine (Israel). Because of competition with humans and domesticated animals, Asiatic asses now live in a few areas isolated from one another.

The kiang lives on the high Tibetan plateau at elevations as high as 4,800 meters (16,000 feet). The kiang is the largest wild ass, 142 centimeters (57 inches) at the shoulder, as tall as a small horse. Its strong body is marked by a heavy head and thick neck, with long legs ending with broad hooves. In the summertime,

The African wild ass is a lovely animal, with its graceful ears and delicate leg stripes. This mare is living with her year-old foal and her two-year-old.

kiangs sport a beautiful bright red-brown coat with a browner long, thick coat in winter to protect them from the cold. The belly and legs of the kiang are white, with the white reaching up onto the sides of the neck and body, and onto the muzzle. There is a white ring around each eye, and the insides of the ears are white.

These handsome animals live in both small and large herds. The males, or some males, appear to live alone for much of the year. Since no one has done a careful study of Asiatic wild ass behavior, we do not know the details of their social life. Apparently, a distinct mating season occurs during the late summer, and the males take over bands of females and defend them against other males. Stallions engage in spectacular fights over the females. The foals are born in mid-summer and apparently stay with the mother for two years.

Onagers

The onager has been a part of human history for centuries, for it was possibly the first equid to be domesticated. The ancient Sumerians used onagers to pull chariots as early as 2,500 B.C. Horses may have been domesticated before this time, but there is no direct evidence. Onagers used to live all across the deserts and steppes of Asia, from the Gobi desert across into northern India and northern Arabia. Now, because of competition with humans, these wily desert creatures live in only four small areas.

The kulan, also called the Mongolian wild ass, lives today on the deserts of central Asia. There are fewer and fewer of these most fleet-footed of all equids every year. In 1968 there were estimated to be only about 750 kulang left in the wild. The Gobi desert, with its treeless plains dotted by harsh vegetation, is the typical habitat of the kulan. This equid is similar in coloration to the kiang but with smaller white areas and often a less reddish summer coat.

The kulan has incredible stamina. In 1925, the naturalist Roy Chapman Andrews observed kulans in the Gobi desert. He chased one stallion for 46 kilometers

The kulan is a swift Asiatic wild ass.

ZOOLOGICAL SOCIETY OF SAN DIEGO

(29 miles) with a car before the animal had to stop. The ability of kulans to sprint at 64 kilometers per hour (40 mph) allows them to escape from their enemies, the desert wolves, whose top speed is 58 kilometers per hour (36 mph).

The khur, or Indian wild ass, has a grayish tan to reddish gray coat in summer and a gray to pale red winter coat. The winter coat is short, for the climate is milder where this equid lives. Like other Asiatic wild asses, the Indian variety is becoming more scarce every year. While there were from 3,000 to 5,000 animals in 1956, by 1969 there appeared to be only 400.

The smallest Asiatic wild ass is extinct today. The Syrian onager, which stood only about 100 centimeters (40 inches) at the shoulder, was the wild ass of the Bible. Once found over a wide area of Middle Eastern desert, these dainty-hooved, slender equids were already scarce by the turn of the century. The last animal died in a Vienna zoo in 1927.

The Burro

Donkey, burro, ass—all three names refer to the same patient servant, the domesticated ass. While scientists agree that this useful and hardy creature is descended from the African ass, they disagree about just which variety or varieties it came from. The ancient Egyptians were the first to domesticate asses, and they have been servants of civilization ever since. Burros come in many sizes and colors. The tiny Sicilian burro may be only 60 centimeters (24 inches) tall at the shoulder, while donkeys from the Spanish island of Majorca are sometimes taller than 155 centimeters (62 inches) in shoulder height. Most burros are gray or tan in their basic body color, but white, black, dark brown, and even pinto burros also exist. White burros have been considered special by many civilizations.

In the United States, there are many populations of feral burros. Like the horses, feral burros have presented a problem for people. Ranchers say they compete with domesticated stock for food and that they foul waterholes, and some wildlife biologists feel they compete with bighorn sheep. But animal lovers want to protect the wild burros. The same laws that protect wild horses protect the burros as well, and many burros have been captured and adopted, just like the horses.

Patricia Moehlman studied the behavior of feral burros in Death Valley, California. Wild burro society appears to be much like that of African asses. The only long-term relationship seems to be between the mother and her foal, but larger groups may stay together for a few days near water. Young animals may group together now and then. Some feral burro males have territories and some do not. The territories are small, but otherwise are like those of African asses and Grevy's zebras. The male burro allows other burros on his

BUREAU OF LAND MANAGEMENT

These excess wild burros have been rounded up and will soon be picked up by the people who have adopted them.

territory, but only he can mate within its boundaries. In areas where no male has staked a claim, other burros can mate.

Burros have very expressive voices. Their famous bray, which can be heard two miles away, can convey many meanings. Males, like roosters, may bray soon after dawn as if announcing the new day. They also bray in greeting or in threat or as part of courting. The soft bray of a lost foal brings its mother to its side. Burros also grunt, growl, and snort to communicate with one another, and a peculiar "whuffle" sound is used by the female while searching for her foal.

Mules—Made-to-Order Workers

Mules are produced by breeding a horse mare with a donkey stallion. The resulting foal has good traits from both parents. It is stronger than either horses or donkeys. Its narrow, donkey-like hooves make it sure-footed even when heavily burdened. A pack mule may carry a load equal to almost half its weight as far as 40 kilometers (25 miles) in a day. While mules have a reputation for stubbornness, they are generally co-operative and gentle animals which prefer to lead rather than to be led. Most mules are a uniform dark color—black, brown, or dark gray—but some are almost white. They lack the light facial markings and light belly of the donkey as well as the back and shoulder stripes.

Mules may have been bred as long as 3,000 years ago and were used in Biblical lands before 1,000 B.C. The donkey had been considered the royal beast before then, but mules took over that honored position. Mules were also bred in ancient Greece at about the same time and were used as work animals as well as in chariot races. It may seem hard to imagine a mule racing, since our image of them is as laden pack animals or patient wagon pullers. But mules were fleet enough to pull Olympic chariots for at least 50 years.

Mules, like most hybrid animals, are almost always

sterile. No male mule is known to have produced off-spring, but about one in 200,000 female mules does become pregnant from a stallion. During the years between 1932 to 1943, five mule foals were recorded.

A donkey mare can also be bred with a horse stallion; the resulting hybrid is called a hinny. Hinnies are more horse-like than mules. Hinnies are bred more rarely than mules, partly because female donkeys do not become pregnant as easily as mares.

Eight

Horse Relatives, Ancient and Modern

Horses, zebras, and asses are all so closely related that they can interbreed, and all look very similar. What other animals are related to horses? Cows and deer have hooves, too—where do they fit in? To sort out the relationships between horses and other animals, we must go way back to the Paleocene period, about 70 million years ago. By that time, dinosaurs had died out and left the world to the early mammals. Condylarths were primitive mammals which gave rise to all later plant-eating mammals. These creatures were so unspecialized in structure that it is difficult to describe them. They had five toes with hooves, long bodies and tails, and relatively short legs. These unassuming creatures were the ancestors of pigs, antelope, giraffes, whales, elephants, aardvarks, horses, and many other mammals.

Different sorts of condylarths evolved into different kinds of mammals. One type led to horses, rhinoceroses, and tapirs, the animal group given the tongue-twist-

Condylarths, which were the ancestors of both odd- and even-toed ungulates, probably looked something like this. DRAWING BY THE AUTHOR

ing name "Perissodactyla," (per-iso-dak'-tila), meaning "odd-toed" ungulates. Another sort of condylarth gave rise to the "Artiodactyla," meaning "even-toed" ungulates, such as pigs, deer, cows, and antelope. Way back many millions of years ago, this key difference between the two sorts of ungulates had already shown up. While horses carry their weight on one toe (derived from the third condylarth toe), cows and other artiodactyls bear their weight on two toes (corresponding to the third and fourth toes of condylarths). Tapirs and rhinos have three toes instead of one, but even they carry most of their weight on the enlarged middle toe. Some artiodactyls, such as camels and giraffes, have only two toes while others, including pigs and deer, have

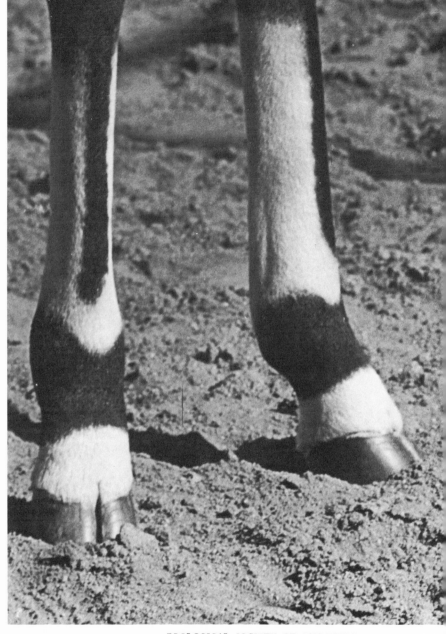

Artiodactyls carry their weight on an even number of toes. The "cloven hooves" of this okapi are a good example.

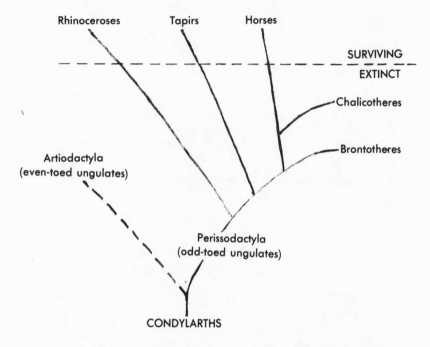

The ancient condylarths gave rise to all ungulates. This simplified diagram shows the perissodactyls mentioned in this book. Actually, as many as 17 different lines of perissodactyls evolved. Only three—horses, tapirs, and rhinos—survive today.
DRAWING BY THE AUTHOR

four. But even artiodactyls with four toes carry their weight on the larger middle two. Because of this "split" foot, artiodactyls are known as "cloven-hooved" mammals.

Ancient Relatives

Today there are only three surviving families of perissodactyls—the horse, rhinoceros, and tapir families. But in prehistoric times, eleven or more other families roamed the earth. Some of these were strange creatures indeed.

The brontotheres were huge animals which lived in North America and Eurasia. They were as tall as 2½ meters (8 feet) at the shoulder and had a big branched horn on top of their noses. They had elephant-like feet and heavy bodies. The brontotheres became suddenly and mysteriously extinct not long after having evolved into many different species.

More mysterious than the brontotheres were the chalicotheres. Chalicotheres had longer front legs than hind legs, giving their backs a peculiar sloping look. Some of them were larger than the largest modern horses. The strangest thing about these long-gone creatures was their feet. Instead of having hooves protecting their toes, the chalicotheres had huge claws which could be moved up and down like those of cats. When the first fossil feet of these peculiar animals were found, paleontologists believed that they were from some giant scaly anteater or ground sloth. Only when a complete skeleton with the feet in their natural position was found, could anyone believe that those feet went with that skeleton.

The combination of large-clawed feet and plant-eating teeth appeared in two other sorts of extinct hooved animals as well. But no animal alive today has this particular combination of characteristics, so no one can be sure just how these creatures lived. Possibly the strong claws were used to dig up roots or tubers which provided the chief food for chalicotheres. Or maybe the claws were used as hooks to pull food down from overhead branches. The life style of these animals is one of the most interesting puzzles in paleontology.

Living Fossils

Looking at a tapir is like peering through a window in time. These rotund creatures have changed little in 40 million years. One look at a tapir's feet, with the four-toed front feet and three-toed hind feet gives away their closeness to the very first perissodactyls such as eohippus. While many species of tapirs and tapir-like creatures once populated the earth, only four species remain today. Before geologists had proof that South America and Asia were connected long ago, biologists had trouble explaining why tapirs were found only in Asia and tropical America. Now it is easy to understand. When the two continents became separated millions of years ago, these ancient animals just stayed where they were and kept on surviving.

Tapirs are about the size of a donkey—75 to 100 centimeters (30 to 40 inches) tall at the shoulder. They look rather like pigs at first glance, with their rounded bodies and somewhat short legs and short tails. Tapirs have small eyes and rounded ears. The American spe-

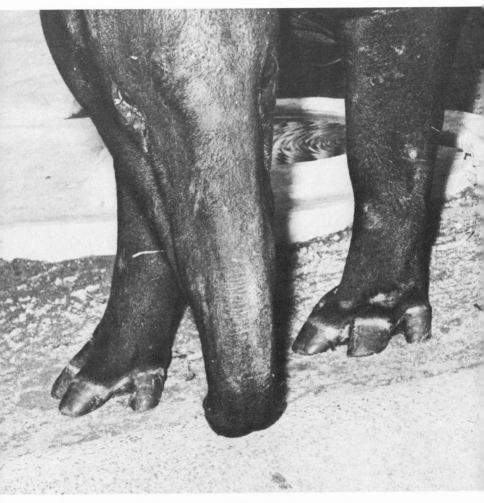

Tapirs use their sensitive snouts to sniff the ground. Their front feet have four toes, each with its own hoof. Only three of the four toes show here.

cies have short manes along the tops of their necks, and all have a long, sensitive snout which extends over the mouth like a trunk. All baby tapirs have an interesting pattern of white or yellowish stripes and dots which they lose when they are about six months old. Some biologists believe this sort of pattern is similar to that of extinct relatives such as eohippus.

The Malayan tapir is the largest species. It lives in southeastern Asia. Its white body has blackish legs, shoulders, neck, and head. It lacks a distinct mane. When lying down to rest during the day, the Malayan tapir, with its light and dark colors, looks like a pile of rocks. The wars in southeast Asia and jungle clearing

The Malayan tapir has a unique color pattern which helps camouflage it in its natural habitat.   LOS ANGELES ZOO

Baird's tapir is rapidly disappearing in the wild, and only a few live in zoos.

for agriculture have destroyed much of this animal's home and many fear its extinction. The Malayan tapir can survive and even reproduce in zoos, but not very many live in captivity at present.

The Brazilian, or lowland, tapir is the most common variety. It lives in the forests of Brazil, Paraguay, and northern Argentina. This species thrives in zoos and will reproduce in captivity. Baird's tapir, which is the largest wild mammal found in the American tropics, lives in Mexico and Central America, and the western parts of Colombia and Ecuador. Baird's tapir is on the endangered species list and is rapidly losing the battle for survival against civilization. Few of these appealing animals live in zoos, but they do well there.

The mountain tapir lives in the Andes at elevations of 2,000 to 4,000 meters (6,500 to 13,000 feet). The soft, woolly coat of the mountain tapir protects it against the cold mountain air. Its fur is especially thick on the underside, where the hairs may be several centimeters long. The mountain tapir is also an endangered species, but unfortunately this unique animal does not live well in zoos. It seems to have trouble adapting to lowland climates. Hardly anything is known about the behavior of the mountain tapir, and soon it may be gone for good.

Tapirs in general like to live in forested areas near the water. Their low, wedge-shaped bodies are well-suited to moving through thick underbrush. Strangely enough, tapirs are strong swimmers and may dive into the water to escape predators, or to feed on water plants. They eat leaves, small branches, and tender sprouts out of the water as well as in it. While they have poor eyesight, tapirs have especially sensitive noses. Their flexible trunks are constantly twitching, extending, and contracting as the animals sniff their way along in the search for food. They can also use

LOS ANGELES ZOO

The mountain tapir has a thick, woolly coat even as a baby to protect it from the cold mountain air.

their trunks to grab onto branches and pull them down. Tapirs are not at all social. Rarely do more than two animals, a mother with her young, travel together. In zoos, when they are confined together in a small enclosure, tapirs get along fine together, but they pay little attention to one another.

While tapir meat is said to be not very tasty, tapirs are hunted for their hides. All but the mountain tapir have smooth, slick coats covering very tough skin, well suited for life in the scratchy jungle underbrush. Natives like to use tapir hides for making reins and whips.

If you see a tapir in a zoo, you will be amazed at just how much the living tapir foot resembles the reconstructed eohippus foot. There are four toes with small hooves on the forefoot, just as in eohippus. The middle toe is the largest and strongest, but the second and fourth toes also touch the ground. The small fifth toe is very short and touches the ground only when it is soft. The back foot has only three toes. Again, the middle toe is the strongest and longest.

Giants from the Past

Rhinoceroses have been around since the early days of perissodactyls, and some have changed little in three million years. The largest known land mammal ever to live was a gigantic rhinoceros which stood 5.4 meters (18 feet) at the shoulder. Rhinos have an ancient look to them with their awkward, heavy bodies, thick hides, and horned noses. The name "rhinoceros" means "nose-horn" in Greek. Actually, a rhino's horn is quite different from cow, goat, or antelope horn. It grows from the skin rather than from bone. The only sign of the horn on the skull is a very roughened area of bone to which the horn is anchored. The horn keeps growing throughout the life of the animal and is kept smooth and shiny by constant use in digging and rubbing. All rhinos, except most females of the Javan species, have one or two horns.

Despite their large size, most rhinos are quite timid. They have poor eyesight but well-developed senses of hearing and smell. Rhinos may not look much like horses, but they use their three-toed feet to walk, trot, and gallop just like horses. Each toe is protected by a wide, hoof-like nail, and the third (middle) toe is the biggest and strongest, just as in horses and tapirs.

The massive size and thick skin of rhinos make them look like living tanks. These two white rhinos are not about to give an inch.   SATOUR

Rhinos of Asia

Three species of rhino live in Asia. The Sumatran rhino may be too far gone to save; there are probably only 50 to 150 of these two-horned, smooth-skinned animals left. Sumatran rhinos are solitary creatures which use their flexible lips to browse on leaves, twigs, fruits, and bamboo shoots.

The Great Indian or One-horned rhinoceros is the most abundant Asian rhino today, with over 1,000 animals surviving and well-protected. This huge animal weighs in at 2,000 to 4,000 kilograms (4,400 to 8,800 pounds) and may be two meters (78 inches) tall at the shoulder. The almost hairless skin has strange horny bumps and peculiar loose folds which give it an armor-like look.

Indian rhinos live a solitary life, preferring to stay near the water where they can take a daily swim. The single calf is born 19 months after mating and may weigh as much as 75 kilograms (165 pounds) at birth. The calf stays with its mother for two years before setting out on its own. All rhinos have similar slow rates of reproduction, which is one reason for their rapid decline in the wild.

The Lesser One-horned or Javan rhino once lived over an extensive range in Asia, from India and Sikkim to China, Sumatra, and Java. Now it has been reduced to one population of only about 50 animals in a Javan preserve, with perhaps a handful of animals still living in nearby jungles. This animal is similar to the Indian rhino but is much smaller. It has small, flattened, horny disks on its skin instead of bumps.

Rhinos in Africa

Two kinds of rhinos live in Africa, the black rhino and the white rhino. The names are quite confusing, for both species are dark in color. The white rhino's name is derived from the Afrikaans (Dutch) word *weit*—meaning "wide"—which refers to its wide, square muzzle. Because of its squared-off upper lip, it is also called the square-lipped rhino. The black rhino has a flexible, pointed upper lip which hangs down somewhat over the lower lip. Both kinds have two horns.

The differences in the lips reflect very different ways of feeding. Black rhinos use their flexible upper lip to grab onto branches and pull down leaves. The white rhino feeds by browsing on grasses. The white rhino is perhaps the largest animal feeding purely on grass which ever evolved, with some adult males reaching 3,600 kilograms (almost four tons) in weight.

The black rhino, like its Asian cousins, is generally solitary. The mother and her calf stay together, and males apparently stake out territories which they mark

The black rhino has a flexible, pointed upper lip which it uses to grasp its food.

with dung heaps and sticks on which they rub their bodies. Black rhinos can be dangerous animals, for they sometimes charge towards a disturbing smell or sound. Despite their clumsy-looking bodies, these living tanks can run headlong towards an enemy, imagined or real, at speeds up to 45 kilometers per hour (22 mph). They use their horns in defense and can easily toss a person into the air or seriously damage an automobile.

White rhinos are more sociable than other kinds. As

White rhinos have square lips. They are probably the largest grass-eating animals ever to inhabit the earth.

a matter of fact, their social life is quite similar to that of Grevy's zebras. Males stake out large breeding territories and challenge one another at the boundaries. Females, calves, and nonbreeding males are all tolerated by the territorial males. Females and calves may gather together in casual groups of six or more individuals, while groups as large as 30 may congregate at a waterside. The cows and young animals seem to prefer to be with others of their kind, for solitary cows or immature males are rarely seen.

The Disappearing Rhinos

The world's rhinos may be fighting a losing battle with extinction. The five species of living rhinos today make up a total of only about 20,000 to 30,000 individual animals. While an estimated 20,000 black rhinos inhabited Kenya ten years ago, now only 1,000 to 1,500 remain. The same story is being repeated in other countries. Dr. Lee Talbot, one of the world's few rhino experts, believes that 90% of Africa's rhinos have been killed during the last five years. Some Asian rhinos are disappearing even faster.

Why are people killing off rhinos at such an alarming rate? Rhinos, with their gigantic bodies and impressive horns, have always been looked upon with awe. There are people who consider them to have magical properties, with different parts of their bodies considered as useful for treating many different human ailments. Charts showing which part of the rhino will cure what disease are found all over the Orient. While a rhino's blood, teeth, hair, skin, and internal organs are believed by some to be good for what ails you, its horn is thought to be even better. Powdered rhino horn supposedly cures measles, food poisoning, diphtheria, drug overdoses, and assorted other ailments. And there are those who believe it to be a powerful love potion as well. When mixed with herbs, it is supposed to eliminate boils and chicken pox if applied to the skin. Rhino horns are also carved into beautiful dagger handles which are a traditional gift in the Middle East when a boy becomes a man. These daggers, when elaborately carved and decorated, may sell for as much as $12,000. A carver can make four dagger handles from one rhino horn. Then he can grind up the scraps and sell the powder to Chinese herb dealers.

Saving the Rhinos

Fortuntely, the governments of most countries where rhinos live are eager to save them, for rhinos are as effective as tourist attractions as they are believed by some to be in herbal medicines. The World Wildlife Fund has launched a "Save the Rhino" campaign, and many countries are cooperating. Kenya has declared an end to all rhino hunting and trade in rhino products, and other African countries are willing to help, too. Asian countries, such as Thailand and Nepal, are also interested in saving the rhinos and have set up preserves where the animals are protected. The most difficult problem for these countries to solve, however, is that of poachers who hunt rhinos illegally and are willing to kill game wardens who try to stop them.

The Problem of Extinction

Every group of perissodactyls—horses, tapirs, and rhino—face the same threat of extinction. Tarpans, quaggas, and Syrian onagers are already gone, while Nubian asses and Przewalski horses have almost certainly disappeared in the wild. It is probably too late to save the Sumatran rhino, and the remaining populations of Cape mountain zebras and Javan rhinos are pitifully small compared to their former numbers.

Throughout time, humans have not respected the animals with which they share the world. As long as 8,000 years ago, people may have contributed significantly to the extinction of horses in the Americas. And still to this day, the poachers who kill rhinos and the hunters who chase wild asses across the desert for sport are threatening to eliminate animals which have caused them no harm. The continuing growth of human populations, which requires ever more land for housing and agriculture, keeps restricting the land available to wildlife.

Once a species is gone it cannot be brought back to life. Scientists may try to "recreate" extinct animals as they have done with the tarpan and the steppe tarpan, but rarely is even such an attempt possible. Before it is too late, humans must realize that the earth is ours to share with other living things, not ours to own. What would the world be like today if horses had not crossed over into Europe and Asia, if all horses had disappeared when American horses died out? No thoroughbreds to race, no cow horses to herd cattle, no work horses to help farmers, no pleasure horses to bring joy to us all.

Biologists fear that by the end of this century a million more species of plants and animals, large and small, will become extinct because of human interference with the natural world. If these gloomy predictions prove correct, the world will be a far less varied and wonderful place in which to live.

Glossary

artiodactyl: An even-toed ungulate, such as a cow or pig, which carries its weight mainly on the second and fourth toes.

eohippus: The "dawn horse," eohippus is the earliest known horse-like animal. Horses, tapirs, and rhinos are all descended from this animal, scientifically called Hyracotherium, which lived about 60 million years ago.

equid: A member of the family Equidae.

Equidae: The horse family, including horses, asses, and zebras.

feral: Wild, but either once tamed or descended from tame animals.

incisors: The front teeth, used by horses to nip off bunches of grass.

kiang: A variety of the Asiatic ass found in the Himalayas.

kulan: A variety of Asiatic ass which lives in the Gobi desert; also called the Mongolian wild ass.

molars: The back teeth, used for grinding and crushing food.

onager: A type of Asiatic ass; the name onager often includes all Asiatic asses except the kiang.

perissodactyl: A member of the order Perissodactyla, which includes equids, rhinos, tapirs, and many extinct animals which have an odd number of weight-bearing toes.

premolars: The teeth in front of the molars. In horses, the premolars look like the molars and are used as they are, for grinding food.

species: A species includes similar animals which will breed with one another in nature; often it is difficult to determine whether populations of animals belong to the same species or not.

ungulate: A convenient grouping rather than a scientific word. It is used to refer to the artiodactyls and perisodactyls together.

Suggested Reading

Books

Lois Darling and Louis Darling, *Sixty Million Years of Horses* (Morrow, N.Y., 1960).

Colin P. Groves, *Horses, Asses, and Zebras in the Wild* (Ralph Curtis Books, Hollywood, Fla. 1974).

Alice L. Hopf, *Wild Cousins of the Horse* (Putnam's, N.Y., 1977).

Sigmund A. Lavine and Vincent Scuro, *Wonders of Donkeys* (Dodd, Mead, N.Y., 1978).

Sigmund A. Lavine and Brigid Casey, *Wonders of Ponies* (Dodd, Mead, N.Y., 1980).

Dorcas MacClintock and Ugo Mochi, *A Natural History of Zebras* (Scribner's, N.Y., 1976).

Dorcas MacClintock and Ugo Mochi, *Horses as I See Them* (Scribner's, N.Y., 1980).

Hope Ryden, *America's Last Wild Horses* (Dutton, N.Y., revised edition, 1978).

Jack Denton Scott, *Island of Wild Horses* (Putnam's, N.Y., 1978). About the wild ponies of Assateague Island.

Robert Vavra, *Such Is the Real Nature of Horses* (Morrow, N.Y., 1979). A beautiful book with over 300 color photos of horses being themselves, accompanied by a text with much information about horse behavior.

Morris Weeks, *The Last Wild Horse* (Houghton Mifflin, Boston, 1977). About the Przewalski horse.

Magazine Articles

Emily and Per Ola d'Aulaire, "Is This the Creature Time Forgot?" *International Wildlife,* Jan.-Feb. 1979. About tapirs.

G. Blair, "Burro Problem at Grand Canyon," *National Parks and Conservation Magazine,* March 1978.

R. D. Estes, "Zebras Offer Clues to the Way Horses Once Lived," *Smithsonian,* Nov. 1974.

P. Des Roses Moehlman, "Getting to Know the Wild Burros of Death Valley," *National Geographic,* April 1972.

Hope Ryden, "Return of the Native; Wild Mustangs," *National Parks and Conservation Magazine,* Oct. 1971.

Hope Ryden and Dick Durrance II, "On the Track of the West's Wild Horses," *National Geographic,* Jan. 1971.

Theodore H. Savory, "The Mule," *Scientific American,* Dec. 1970.

Hans Silvester, "Wild and Free," *International Wildlife,* Jan.-Feb. 1977. About the horses of the Camargue.

A. Sirdofsky, "Pony Penning on Chincoteague Island," *Travel/ Holiday,* June 1979.

Joseph Stocker, "Battle of the Burro," *National Wildlife,* Aug.-Sept. 1980.

Index

Adopt-a-Horse program, 38, 39-40
Anchitherium, 27, 28
Andrews, Roy Chapman, 91-92
Artiodactyla, 98-99, 100, 119
ass, African, 68, 86-88, 89, 92, 93; Asiatic, 88-92; Indian, 92; Mongolian, 91; Nubian, 87, 116; Somali, 87; see also burro, kiang, kulan, onager
Assateague Island, 56, 57

bachelor (stallion) groups, in horses, 42; in zebras, 69, 73, 74
bacteria, 16
Barbs, 33
binocular vision, 12
bit, 14
bones, 14, 16-18, 22-23
brontotheres, 100, 101
burros, 92-94; bray of, 94; feral, 39, 93-94; Majorcan, 93; Sicilian, 93

Camargue, horses, 54-55
camels, 98
canine teeth, 14, 15
cecum, 15-16
cellulose, 16
cement of teeth, 15, 29, 30

chalicotheres, 100, 101-102
Chincoteague ponies, 55-57
colon, 15-16
communication, in burros, 94; in horses, 48-49; in zebras, 68
condylarths, 97, 98
Coronado, 34

Dales pony, 57
deer, 98-99
dentine, 30
dewlap, 79
donkey, 92; see also burro
dusting, 44, 47

ears, 12-13, 67
Egyptians, 92-93
elephants, 20
enamel of teeth, 15, 29, 30
enzymes, 16
Eocene, 24-25, 27
eohippus, 21-24, 27, 108, 119
Epihippus, 25, 27
Equidae, 10-11, 119
Equus, 27, 31
evolution, of domestic horses, 59-62; of horses, 19-32; process of, 20-21
Exmoor pony, 59

Extinction of horses in America, 32
eyes, 12, 30

family bands, horses, 42-44; zebras, 69-72, 73, 74, 75-76
feeding of horses, 13-16
Feist, James, 42, 44
femur, 16
feral, definition of, 37, 119; horses, 36-59; *see also* burros, feral; mustangs
fetlock, 18
fighting, in asses, 90; in horses, 45-46; in zebras, 83, 85
foals, horse, 46-47, 49-51, 61; zebra, 70, 72
foot of horse, 18, 31; of chalicotheres, 101; of tapirs, 102, 103; *see also* hooves, toes
fossils, 21-22, 24, 100

giraffes, 98
grass, 13, 51
Greece, ancient, 95
grinding teeth, 25, 26; *see also* molars, premolars
grooming, 47-48

head, 11, 26
Highland ponies, 47, 58
hinnies, 99
hooves, 18, 22, 31, 97, 103; cloven, 99, 100
humerus, 16
hunting dogs, wild, 75-76
Hypohippus, 27, 28
Hyracotherium, 21, 22, 27; *see also* eohippus

incisors, 13, 14, 119
Indians, 32, 34-35
island ponies, 55-57

Johnston, Velma, 37-39

khur, 92
kiang, 86, 88-90, 119
Klingel, Dr. Hans, 69, 72, 84-85, 87-88
knee, 16
Koniks, 60-62
kulan, 1, 86, 91-92, 119

legs, 11, 16-18, 22-23, 26, 30-31, 88, 97; horse and human compared, 17
Lewis and Clark, 35

Mammalia, 19
mammoths, 20
mares: asses as mothers, 89, 94; horses as mothers, 46-47; horse, rank in family band, 53; zebras as mothers, 70; zebra, rank in family band, 72
McCullough, Dale, 42
Merychippus, 29-31
Mesohippus, 26, 27
Miocene, 26-31
Miohippus, 26, 27, 29, 30
Moehlman, Patricia, 93
molars, 14, 15, 25, 26, 119; *see also* grinding teeth
Mountain Zebra National Park, 80
mules, 95-96
mustangs, 8, 36, 42-51

neck, 11, 23
nicker, 48-49

Oligocene, 25-26, 27, 28
onager, 88, 90-92, 119; Syrian, 92, 116

Paleocene, 97
Perissodactyla, 98, 100, 119
pigs, 98-99
Polish horses, 60-62
ponies, British, 47, 57-59
premolars, 14, 15, 25, 26, 119-120
Pryor Mountain Wild Horse Range, 38, 42, 45, 53
Przewalski horses, 50, 60, 62-64, 116; behavior of, 64

quagga, 76-77, 116

rhinoceroses, 98, 108-116; black (square-lipped), 111-112; feeding of, 111; Great Indian (one-horned), 110; horns of, 108, 111; horns, uses of, 115; Javan (Lesser One-horned), 110-111, 116; lips of, 111, 112, 113; Sumatran, 110, 116; white, 109, 110, 112-114
running, horses adaptations to, 11, 18; by Asiatic asses, 88, 91-92; by black rhinos, 112

Sable Island ponies, 55
Shetland ponies, 57-58
skull, 14
Spanish horses, 33
species, 10, 120
spine, 11, 23
stallion, ass, 88, 90; horse, 42-46; zebra, 71, 72, 73, 78, 82-85; *see also* bachelor (stallion) groups
stripes, zebra, 65, 68
Sumarians, 90

tail, 23
tapirs, 98, 102-108; Baird's, 105-106; Brazilian (lowland), 105; Malayan, 104-105; mountain, 106, 107; snout (trunk) of, 103, 104, 106
tarpan, 60, 62, 116, 117; forest, 60-62; steppe, 60, 117
teeth, 13-15, 20, 25, 26, 29, 30, 101; *see also* specific kinds
territories, breeding, 82-85, 88, 93
threat behavior, horses, 44, 46, 49
toes, 18, 19-20, 22, 23, 24, 26, 31, 97, 98, 99, 101, 102, 108, 109

ungulate, 97-100, 120

whinny, 48
Wild Free-roaming Horse and Burro Act, 39
Wild Horse Annie, 37-39
wild horses, feral, 33-59, feral in U. S. A., 33-40; life of, 41-51; true, 59-64
wolves, desert, 92
World Wildlife Fund, 115

zebra, 10-11, 65-85; birth of, 70; Burchell's, 66, 68, 84; defenses of, 75; Grevy's, 67, 81-85; Grevy's, behavior of, 82-85, 88; mountain, 68, 78-80; mountain, Cape, 79-80; mountain, Hartmann's, 78, 79, 80; plains, 68, 81; plains, family life, 69-76; plains, other names for, 68; voices of, 68